PRAISE FOR *UNSHATTERED*

As someone who has carried the impact of abuse into adulthood, I resonated deeply with the message of *Unshattered*, which is not just about surviving—it's about rising, transforming pain into strength, and creating a ripple of healing that touches generations. It's tender, powerful, and profoundly human.

Leila Reyes, MSW
Author of *Freedom from Shame:*
Trauma, Forgiveness, and Healing from Sexual Abuse

More than a fascinating memoir, *Unshattered* is a wonderful reminder of our extraordinary resilience and ability to say "victim no more" as we write our new story, reframing and transforming shattering trauma and pain into wholeness and passionate purpose.

Jo Ann Towle, M.A.
Author of *Restless Reins,*
My Wild Ride to Recovery and Freedom

Unshattered is a powerful book with graphic detail of trauma and abuse, but more importantly, the author details not just the healing from that trauma, but truly embracing the value of the lessons learned by overcoming the trauma and stepping into an authentic, soulful, and empowered life. Anyone who reflects upon the healing of their own childhood scars will value the way Churchman has not only faced her own journey but has also helped many others do the same. Her perspective of healing generations of deep wounds through her personal work is profoundly beautiful.

Paula Robbins
Author of *Hitchhiking into Recovery:*
A Journey of Connection, Healing, and Hope

In a culture that has become fixated on endlessly decoding and healing trauma after the fact, *Unshattered* offers a radical and refreshing reframe. Through her own raw stories of pain and perseverance,

Emma Churchman reveals that true resilience is in the claiming of the future by breaking the hold of the past. This powerful book brings to light the challenges of growing up in severe dysfunction, but it also frames the narrative that empowerment starts with knowledge and with acknowledging the far-reaching ramifications and residue that family mental illness encompasses. Churchman shows the reader through her painful stories that patterns can either be repeated or interrupted. In her sharing of the details that shaped the personalities of her mother as well as what foreshadowed horrific loss of loved ones to addiction and suicide, she also shows us hope. *Unshattered* is a profound and necessary contribution that restores our ability to be present, grounded, and whole—even when genetics and environment may appear to be against us.

Dr. Karen Parker
Author of *Quantum Wellness:*
Healing Your Mind, Body, and Spirit with Human Design

UNSHATTERED

SURVIVING MY MOTHER'S 123 PERSONALITIES
AND TRANSFORMING A LEGACY OF ABUSE

EMMA M. CHURCHMAN, MDiv

Editor: Sonia Castleberry
Senior Editor: Laurie Knight
Cover Design: Kristina Edstrom

EMP⊙WER
P   R   E   S   S

An Imprint for GracePoint Publishing (www.GracePointPublishing.com)

GracePoint Matrix, LLC
624 S. Cascade Ave, Suite 201
Colorado Springs, CO 80903
www.GracePointMatrix.com
Email: Admin@GracePointMatrix.com

SAN # 991-6032

A Library of Congress Control Number has been requested and is pending.

ISBN: (Paperback) 978-1-966346-07-4
eISBN: 978-1-966346-48-7
Audiobook ISBN: 978-1-966346-59-3

Books may be purchased for educational, business, or sales promotional use.
For distribution queries contact Sales@IPGbook.com
For non-retail bulk order requests contact Orders@GracePointPublishing.com
Printed in U.S.A

OTHER BOOKS BY
EMMA M. CHURCHMAN, MDɪᴠ

The Deep End of Hope in the Wake of Hurricane Helene: 40 Days and Nights of Survival and Transformation

Navigating the Deep End: Resilient Leadership in a Volatile World (2026)

Dear Reader,

You hold in your hands a story of transformation—not just survival, but the deliberate choice to transform pain into purpose, trauma into triumph.

This memoir chronicles a journey through childhood physical, emotional and sexual abuse, domestic violence, suicide, and the complexities of living with a mother who had 123 distinct personalities. But more importantly, it's the story of how I chose to reframe what happened *for* me rather than *to* me.

If you've picked up this book, you likely recognize something of your own story in its pages. You may be seeking not just validation for your pain, but permission for your joy. You may be ready to discover that your greatest wounds can become your greatest strengths.

The path from shattered to unshattered isn't easy, but it is possible. Every difficult moment you'll read about led to a breakthrough. Every challenge became a catalyst for growth. Every scar became a source of wisdom.

You are stronger than you know. You are more resilient than you realize. And you have everything within you to not just survive your story, but to transform it into something beautiful.

Welcome to the journey from victim to victor, from broken to unbreakable, from shattered to unshattered.

With hope and transformation,

Emma

Everything that ever happened, happened for me.

For my brothers Bryce, Alex, and Edward.

TABLE OF CONTENTS

NOTE TO READERS 1

INTRODUCTION 3

PART 1
THE BACKSTORY

CHAPTER ONE: SAPHRONA 9

CHAPTER TWO: TRACY.. 13

PART 2
THE ALTERS OF MY CHILDHOOD (1974–1987)

CHAPTER THREE: DEBBY 1 21

CHAPTER FOUR: FIVE AND ALICE 27

CHAPTER FIVE: TEN 31

CHAPTER SIX: DEBBIE 35

PART 3
FAMILY SECRETS (1987–1990)

CHAPTER SEVEN: 24.. 45

CHAPTER EIGHT: DAD 49

CHAPTER NINE: BRYCE.. 57

CHAPTER TEN: ALEX 61

CHAPTER ELEVEN: EDWARD 67

CHAPTER TWELVE: SACRIFICE.. 71

PART 4
RESCUE (1990–1992)

CHAPTER THIRTEEN: JOHN 81

CHAPTER FOURTEEN: ANNA 85

CHAPTER FIFTEEN: DEBBIE SUE 95

CHAPTER SIXTEEN: TWO 99

CHAPTER SEVENTEEN: FRANK 105

CHAPTER EIGHTEEN: DEFIANCE 111

PART 5

RECOVERY (1995–1998)

CHAPTER NINETEEN: RUTH 117

CHAPTER TWENTY: DEBBY 2 121

CHAPTER TWENTY-ONE: DON 125

CHAPTER TWENTY-TWO: RESURRECTION 133

PART 6

RECONSTRUCTION (2002–2014)

CHAPTER TWENTY-THREE: THE PSYCHIC 139

CHAPTER TWENTY-FOUR: QUAKER SHAMAN 153

CHAPTER TWENTY-FIVE: SEMINARY 161

CHAPTER TWENTY-SIX: MINISTRY 169

CHAPTER TWENTY-SEVEN: MIDWIFE FOR THE HOLY 175

CHAPTER TWENTY-EIGHT: THE ENTREPRENEUR 183

PART 7

EVOLUTION (2019–2024)

CHAPTER TWENTY-NINE: JEFF 195

CHAPTER THIRTY: SAVED 207

CHAPTER THIRTY-ONE: CRUCIFIXION 219

CHAPTER THIRTY-TWO: CHURCHWOOD 229

CHAPTER THIRTY-THREE: VITALITY 239

CHAPTER THIRTY-FOUR: MOM 243

POSTSCRIPT 251

CONTINUE YOUR HEALING JOURNEY 259

ACKNOWLEDGMENTS 261

ABOUT THE AUTHOR 263

NOTE TO READERS

For most of my life, I was a fragment of a person. We all were, really. Me, my three younger brothers, our mother (Debby), and our father. We all existed in reaction to trauma or abuse or both. None of us were fully formed. Like pieces of a shattered mirror, we reflected distorted versions of ourselves back to each other, each shard containing only a small piece of who we might have been.

Debby was the most shattered of us. She was not a single person but instead a constellation of selves, a universe of fractured identities housed in one body, the legacy of horrific abuse suffered as a child. She was the woman we called mother, and she was also a collective of 123 personalities. A dozen of them occupied daily life throughout my childhood, most were too young to function in our family or in an adult body, and with the exception of one, all were female.

These personalities existed in two distinct realms: "Inside," in Debby's brain, where they lived and took turns emerging, and "Outside," where they physically manifested in Debby's body, visible to those around her. Some became as familiar to us as family members while others remained mysterious, appearing briefly before retreating back Inside, leaving us to wonder which version of our mother we might encounter next.

Growing up as the child of a multiple, never knowing from one minute to the next who I was speaking to and what they knew about what was happening in that moment, was a jarring experience. One minute I'd be speaking with someone in Debby's body about what we were having for dinner, and the next minute, that person was gone, replaced with someone who had no idea it was dinnertime and was more interested in being left alone to smoke cigarettes. Two minutes later a small child would pop Out, wanting to play. Each personality brought its own memories, its own version of reality, its own needs and demands that we had to navigate while trying to maintain some semblance of normal life.

The switching of Debby's personalities was constant in our household, and this book reflects that disjointed upbringing. But it also chronicles how that very fragmentation led me to become whole, first as a trauma chaplain in a hospital, where I learned to sit with others in their darkest moments, and now as a trauma chaplain and mentor helping others navigate their own trauma recovery and journey toward resilience. What once felt like a curse—growing up with a mother of split personalities—became the foundation for my life's work: helping others find their way back to themselves after trauma.

This book is more than a memoir of growing up with a mother of multiple personalities. It's a testament to the human spirit's capacity for survival, adaptation, resilience, and ultimately, transformation. It's about how we can take the very things that broke us into a million pieces and use them to help ourselves and others heal. It's about finding wholeness in the fragments, purpose in the pain, and hope in the spaces in between.

INTRODUCTION

Debby, my mother, is an exceptional storyteller. She writes stories professionally as a journalist for well-known newspapers, most of them about things for kids to do around our hometown of Washington, DC. In her circle of friends, she is always the center of attention at parties.

One fall night in 1986, my three brothers and I are at the center of her attention, the focus of her brilliant storytelling skills. We are her captive audience as we obediently gather in the basement of our house for a movie. It's a rare occurrence in our house. We are only ever allowed to watch TV if it is a preapproved educational show on PBS, such as Sesame Street, The Electric Company, 3-2-1 Contact, *or, my favorite,* Mr. Rogers' Neighborhood™.

Our father remains upstairs, always a loner, even in his own family.

Debby has chosen Quest for Fire *to entertain us on this unseasonably sticky and humid night. Set in Paleolithic Europe 80,000 years ago, the 1982 film focuses on the struggle for control of fire by early humans. A trio of warriors travel the savanna in search of a flame that would replace the fire their tribe lost. Rated R for severe violence, gore, frightening and intense scenes, and for moderate sex and nudity, it somehow made Debby's cut as an educational opportunity.*

We are piled onto a queen-sized futon. Edward, Alex, Bryce, and I are six months and four, ten, and twelve years old, respectively. We fit together easily on the futon, mainly because Edward is napping in my lap. Remarkably, he isn't awake and crying, which is how he spends most of his time, giving voice to our family's internal battles.

The futon is covered with a blue, fitted bedsheet to hide the stains and memories of the past. Remnants of Alex's drawing with permanent markers streak the wooden arms. I make a mental note of the unexplained bloodstain on the sheet beside my left arm.

Debby is seated next to us in an old wooden rocking chair inherited from her grandmother. She has haphazardly re-covered its cushions with thick gray, green, and maroon-flowered upholstery, adhering it to the rocking chair with a gray braided upholstery edge and brass tacks.

We never have nice furniture in our house. Even this antique rocking chair with its newer upholstery is hard to look at because in many places the upholstery doesn't stretch far enough to meet the tacks, leaving the edges jagged. It is a violent betrayal of the original design. I am glad it lives in the basement, so guests won't see it.

I hate being down here. It is brutal and dank. For respite, and if you are careful, you can crank open the small, high windows. We never do though because one time Bryce tried to and the window broke. Our father beat him until he cried.

I recall that we pulled the new carpet up from the basement floor shortly after we moved in the year before—after it had flooded a few times, leaving the carpet perpetually moldy. The door to the outside is hung a little high, leaving a two-inch gap between the floor and the bottom of the door. Every time it rains, water flows in. No one thinks to clean the outdoor drain of leaves or to fix the door to prevent flooding.

We are never protected, even when the door is closed.

When we removed the carpet, we found stained and chipped black-and-white tile; clearly the carpet had been installed to hide this. Flecked with red, green, and blue, the tile must have been pretty when it was first laid. Debby put me in charge of refinishing the floor a few months ago, having me install shiny peel-and-stick vinyl tile that mimics oak flooring directly on top of the chipped tile.

I am only twelve; I have no idea what I am doing, so even though I have just installed the new vinyl floor, it is already peeling and coming apart. No one tells me not to install new tile directly on top of old tile. No one shows me how to clean the ceramic tile before glueing the vinyl so the dirt won't prevent the new tile from adhering.

No one tells me what to do.

Water still flows into the basement every time it rains. Only now, it gets stuck between the vinyl and ceramic tile, taking up residence in our already too-crowded house. It squishes when we walk on it, which makes us kids giggle, Dad rage, and Debby freeze.

My brothers and I lose interest three minutes into Quest for Fire. *No character speaks English. Instead, there is a lot of grunting and incoherent mumbling. We can't figure out what's happening.*

Sensing our disinterest, Debby decides to narrate the entire one-hundred-minute film to us, like it is no big deal for her to watch a movie for the first time while simultaneously chronicling the whole thing. She begins speaking over the grunting and mumbling of the movie characters, assuming distinct voices and intonations for different characters.

"Look Fred, there's danger approaching."

"No, Mike, I don't see or smell anything."

Mike, to Fred: "Why are you always disagreeing with me?"

Jake: "Stop arguing you guys and protect the fire."

Eight minutes into the movie, Mike, Fred, and Jake's tribe is under vicious attack by another tribe. A woman is raped. People are brutally killed and then eaten by a pack of wolves.

"I'm having too many feelings about this," says Mike (in Debby's voice). Whining, he cries out, "All of my friends are dead. Our only fire went out. How will we ever survive?"

Mike finally pulls it together enough to fight a group of cannibals and steal their fire, only to get his genitals bitten off. Debby's unfolding narration is entertaining and hysterical, distracting us from the graphic, violent sex scenes, and the perpetual brutality of it all. The older boys and I nudge each other and suppress giggles behind our hands while watching the unfolding horror.

Debby keeps drawing our attention back. In addition to the different voices and intonations, she's now even developing additional plotlines to hold our interest. Like a playwright demanding we watch only her performance, we are imprisoned by her storytelling, held captive in the theater of her imagination.

I now understand that we were trapped in her delusional world, in her fractured mind, where reality was whatever personality took center stage that day.

At the time, I had no conscious awareness that different people lived inside of Debby. I was too busy being mother to my brothers, too focused on managing the daily drama to see the larger performance unfolding. To this day, I'm still not sure which of Debby's alternative identities, or alters, narrated that movie. I now know that the collective, the person we called Debby, had 123 distinct personalities, each with their own character and plot—a full theater company living inside one woman while her children lived in survival mode.

Each alter was like a new freestanding episode in an endless series, with its own rules, its own reality, its own version of motherhood. While I was changing diapers, making bottles, and protecting my brothers, Debby was crafting new personalities to avoid the very responsibilities I had been forced to assume. The irony wasn't lost on me later—that while she created multiple selves to escape reality, I had to become multiple things to maintain it: mother, sister, protector, survivor.

PART 1
THE BACKSTORY

CHAPTER ONE

SAPHRONA

The thing about shameful family secrets is that they are either kept secret so no one really knows what happened, and it's all conjecture, or a horrific life is normalized to establish a way to deal with what has happened. My family holds both kinds of secrets.

The story of abuse in my family began with Saphrona, my great-grandmother on my mother's side, and her mother-in-law, Nina. Both women either emotionally or sexually abused Tracy, Debby's mother, my grandmother. Unlike Tracy's abuse of Debby, which was hidden, this abuse became just another family anecdote, like discussing the weather or crop yields. Everyone knew, no one intervened, and the pattern of mothers harming daughters continued unbroken until it reached its crescendo in Debby's multiplicity.

Our family trauma began on the outskirts of Oklahoma City, where Saphrona and her husband built their simple wooden house. Saphrona's parents acquired the 160 acres they farmed during the Oklahoma Land Rush on April 22, 1889. This was the first rush of unassigned lands of former Indian territory, where 50,000 people claimed two million acres in a single day. These 12,000 tracts, originally belonging to the Creek and Seminole peoples, were parceled out under President Lincoln's Homestead Act of 1862. Families could claim up to 160 acres, and if they lived on and improved the land through subsistence farming, they would own it outright in five years.

Saphrona's father illegally acquired the family's premium homestead. The practice in those days was that people could stay with others if they had a lamp on outside their tent. A day or two after the

Land Rush, and before Saphrona was born, her father saw a tent in a place where he wanted to acquire land. Their outside lamp was on. The people, a couple with their young daughter, invited him in and gave him food. As they started talking, they told him, laughing, "You know, we're getting ready to pull a fast one; our daughter is claiming the land next to us, but she's not of age."

So, the next day, Saphrona's father went off to Fort Yukon and claimed that man's daughter's land for himself. He didn't have to do anything other than go into an office to register the land. Others who did what he did came to be called "Sooners," the term used for people who illegally acquired choice tracts of land. Saphrona's father stole the land not only from the Native people but also from fellow White settlers who had journeyed through hardship from the East to claim these free tracts.

Thus began the family trait of doing whatever was necessary to get what was wanted. There was no moral compass, and cheaters, liars, and bastards were rewarded.

The family built a sod house on the property while they saved money to build a wooden home by growing and selling sweet potatoes. My great-grandmother Saphrona was born in the sod house.

The family was dirt-poor, but they eventually scraped together enough money to build a wooden house. They hosted a party to celebrate its completion, but during the party, candles fell over, and the house burned to the ground. So, they returned to living in the sod house for most of Saphrona's childhood.

Later, when Saphrona married, she and her husband built their own family home on this same farm. After her parents died, they called it "Sooner Farm," in honor of the Land Rush. They were also dirt-poor. Saphrona's husband was a truck farmer. He took other farmers' watermelons, corn, and sweet potatoes and sold them in urban areas. Sometimes he bought the fruits and vegetables from the farmers to resell, other times he had his children go into their fields in the middle of the night to steal the produce.

Saphrona and her husband had seven children. Tracy, my grandmother, was the eldest. She was responsible for caring for her younger siblings, including a brother who died on Tracy's watch when he was a toddler. Saphrona blamed Tracy for killing her brother, telling her over and over again that she fouled everything up and referring to her as the black sheep of the family.

Nina, Saphrona's mother-in-law, fell on hard times during the Depression. She went to live with Saphrona and her husband in their tiny house already bursting at the seams with children. One day, Saphrona heard strange sounds coming from Nina's bedroom and walked in on Nina sexually abusing Tracy. Saphrona blew up and immediately threw Nina out. Nothing was ever said about what happened next. It is unknown whether Saphrona comforted Tracy or told her what happened to her was wrong. Given that Tracy always referred to her mother as being "spitfire mean," it is unlikely any compassion was offered.

Perhaps this is how Tracy learned to experience comfort or love. It is conceivable that Nina's sexual abuse was the only form of intimacy Tracy experienced from an older woman, since her own mother had none to give her.

People who experience sexual abuse as children can create an association between love and abuse. The person abused internalizes and rationalizes the emotional and sexual abuse they suffered when they were young. They then perpetuate the cycle of abuse by exploiting others in the same ways they were violated. Sexual abuse often becomes intertwined and confused with love.

Maybe perpetuating sexual abuse is how Tracy took back her power after losing it at such a young age. Perhaps this is how she coped with feelings of inadequacy and insecurity.

Saphrona and Nina emotionally and sexually abused Tracy. Tracy then passed down the abuse to Debby who then gave it to me, creating our own unique maternal lineage, five generations deep and one-hundred years long.

CHAPTER TWO

TRACY

Most pedophiles were abused themselves in childhood. Tracy, my grandmother, perpetuated her lineage of abuse with Debby, carrying our family legacy forward.

One of Debby's earliest memories is of her mother giving her an enema at about age one, a ritual that continued until she was well into elementary school. This is the lightest form of abuse Debby experienced.

Tracy put Debby and her older sister in the bathtub together, calling them "dirty little girls," and placed a long tube with a bag that held water and saline into each of their rectums. She then injected the fluid and left them in the bathtub, disappearing into her bedroom.

I believe this may have been an erotic experience for Tracy, where she would go into her bedroom to masturbate while simultaneously forcing her children to wait for her. Eventually, Debby recalls, the girls would yell out, "We can't hold it anymore!" and Tracy would return and allow them to use the toilet.

This is called *coprophilia*, an erotic fascination with feces and general filth and uncleanliness, and I believe Tracy's obsession was rooted here. It's a sexual fetish where people enjoy coming into contact with feces, where they like the smell, taste, or feel of feces in a sexual way.

This example of coprophilia is the first of many stories I learned of what happened behind closed doors between Tracy and Debby. Debby has alleged that her mother was a rapist and pedophile and sexually abused her for most of her childhood. Debby's sister doesn't recall ever being sexually abused by Tracy. But, decades later, she told me that for her whole life, she felt there was a big secret in their childhood home, and that something was going on she couldn't figure out or see. She told me about writing a story in elementary school about a big secret. There was no explanation of what the secret was because she didn't have one at the time. It was only after Tracy died that the secret of Debby's sexual abuse was exposed.

The day Tracy died of breast cancer, she was an inpatient at the main hospital in Arlington, Virginia, just down the street from where she lived with my grandfather. Tracy's room had two beds, one unoccupied. She was in the bed closest to the window, overlooking the air-conditioning units for the hospital, which were situated on the lower-level roof.

The room had yellow square tiles on the wall and unassuming beige tile on the floor. A chair sat next to Tracy's bed, facing it. I sat in this same chair several times during the previous weeks, with Tracy, whom I called Mimi, attempting to give life advice to me, her eldest grandchild. Education was incredibly important to Tracy—she put herself through college, graduating in 1940, and even paid to have her younger sister attend and graduate from the same women's college. Mimi suggested that I study Latin because she thought it would take me far in life. It was the late 1980s, and I wasn't buying it. She also told me to lose weight so men would like me better.

My mind easily takes me to that moment.

I have just turned thirteen and am excited to enter my teenage years, not yet recognizing that with Tracy's death, I will abruptly enter adulthood.

Today Tracy is in and out of consciousness, and we are taking turns saying goodbye to her. My aunt goes in for her final private visit. Tracy wakes up and grabs my aunt's arm, thinking she is Debby. She whispers, "Don't tell anyone. Don't say anything." My aunt has no idea what Tracy's talking about because at the time neither she nor any other family member has any idea that she sexually abused Debby. Tracy dies a few hours later.

This was Tracy's sole acknowledgment of the past's darkness—a fleeting crack in her fortress of denial. My own story remained buried even deeper, untouched by words or witness. It took thirty-five years and the sanctuary of seminary before these memories surfaced. There, in the most mundane of moments—sitting in a bathroom stall—a childhood scene with Tracy crystallized with devastating clarity, as if time itself had turned transparent, allowing me to finally see what had been hidden in plain sight all along.

When I was a toddler—between eighteen months and two years old—Tracy took care of me while Debby was at work and the sitter who had been watching me suddenly quit without notice or a replacement.

In this memory, Tracy and I are upstairs in the guest bedroom of her house, which has dark wood paneling, cushy white carpet, and low ceilings. It is more like a large attic space, with a tin roof and a tiny bathroom only big enough for a toilet, a minuscule sink, and a shower stall just large enough for a small adult. Hung on the walls on either side of the bed are two beautifully framed family swords. One represents the North, the other the South. Our family was on both sides of the Civil War.

Tracy and I are on the bed, in the middle of the Civil War.

The bedroom is located at the top of a steep, carpeted staircase that leads up from the hallway outside my grandfather's office. The hallway door is closed. The bed has a white popcorn bedspread on it, the same style my parents have on their bed. The sun is streaming onto my face from the windows behind the headboard.

I am lying on my back, and Tracy is putting my feces in my mouth. She is looking down, smiling at me.

My mouth is full of shit, and I can't get it out.

Decades later, I asked Debby if she noticed any changes in me during the time Tracy was caring for me. She said, "I remember thinking that something was off, but then thinking that was because I was just sort of generally irritated with my mother and that I really needed to find somebody else to care for you." She continued, "She would take you to the library and get these nice books and talk to the librarian. She was making an effort."

Then, as if to allay any wrongdoing, she went on to tell me, "To ask an older woman to take care of a very young kid, particularly at that age, is a lot. It's an age in which kids have absolutely no sense, and so you have to follow them carefully everywhere. You can't just plop them in a room and go do the dishes."

In that same conversation, Debby went on to say that she was more concerned about fifty-six-year-old Tracy caring for my younger brother Bryce.

"I vaguely worried about Bryce. Here's why: When I was gonna leave him with her, to run errands or something, I would come to pick him up, and he invariably was missing his pants. Mom would say, 'Well, he wet his pants, and I didn't have any substitutes.' I kinda wondered why this kept happening."

We were never protected, *especially* behind closed doors.

All of Tracy's siblings and their spouses were present at her funeral reception, sucking the air out of the room with their violent cacophony of storytelling and alcohol consumption. The siblings have all "coped" with adulthood in the way their parents and grandparents taught them: Hustle however you can to survive, and wheel and deal so you aren't dirt-poor. The siblings added their own unique spin: Drink yourself into a stupor so you don't have to think about your actions and to numb the feeling that anything is deeply wrong.

At thirteen, I'm drowning in adult chaos. I am surrounded by rooms full of explosive alcoholics—the next iteration of our family's preferred method of fracturing reality. My great-aunts and uncles and their spouses have commandeered the room like a troupe of desperate performers, their voices rising and falling in a violent symphony of grief and gin. Each clutches a drink like a life preserver, their stories growing louder and wilder with every sip, as if volume alone could keep death at bay.

I watch them—these adults who are supposed to show me how to live—and wonder about my future. Is it reflected in their glazed eyes? Their laughter, too loud and sharp-edged, slices through the air, while I stand witness to this preview of inherited destiny, wondering if this is what my life will be when I grow up.

The reception following the funeral was at Tracy and Frank's house. It was an open concept design where the living room flows into the dining room, which flows into the kitchen and the sunroom. They designed and built the house shortly after World War II to host parties, not to raise a family. It was near a prestigious golf course in Arlington, VA, frequented by presidents, just across the river from Washington, DC. Their neighbor across the street was the astronaut

John Glenn. In later years, one of George W. Bush's daughters dated the son of another neighbor up the street. Their neighborhood was wealthy, well-connected, and Republican approved. It represented the economic and social status Tracy fled Oklahoma to attain.

I remember one of my great-uncles held court in my grandfather's favorite chair, positioned like a predator surveying everything happening in the living room, kitchen, and dining room.

He grabs me as I walk by, pulling me onto his lap with the entitled confidence of a man who has never faced consequences, and starts feeling up my ass. I've recently developed breasts and can tell he's going to move to them next. He's laughing the whole time, casually chatting with extended family, holding a drink in one hand and my ass cheek under my dress in the other—performing normalcy while committing atrocity, just as our family has done for generations.

No one seems to notice. Or rather, they choose not to notice. I say nothing because I already know it will fall on deaf ears, just as Saphrona's abuse of Tracy was ignored. I excuse myself and retreat to the creek in the backyard, finding refuge among the rocks.

Decades later, I learned that this great-uncle used his eldest daughter as currency in business deals in the late 1950s and early 1960s, trading her body to men from the time she was eight. He just handed her over and let these men have their way with her.

In this family, your body does not belong to you.

PART 2

THE ALTERS OF MY CHILDHOOD

(1974–1987)

CHAPTER THREE
DEBBY 1

Debby 1 was the alter I believe was present when my brothers and I were born. She was the one who desperately wanted children to love and adore her. She was the one who suffered emotional and physical abuse during her twenty years of marriage to Don, our father, all in the name of having a family to call her own.

My earliest memory is of being rocked by Debby 1, before our home became a house of horrors. It was 1974, and I was six months old. We were sitting on my great-grandmother's yet-to-be-re-covered rocking chair, set in the corner of the living room of our first house, a tiny, white Cape Cod with black shutters in an average neighborhood in Northern Virginia. My parents had just purchased it for $14,000.

I can smell my father's homemade spaghetti sauce wafting from the kitchen on the other side of the wall. Even today I can smell it when I close my eyes. I've made spaghetti sauce hundreds of times in the decades since this memory, yet I have never been able to exactly replicate that smell.

The smell of comfort.

The alter who married my father, Don—whom my brothers and I later call Debby 1—*is patting my back and singing to me. I am wearing a onesie and must have just woken up from a nap.*

When I was a teenager, Debby told me it wasn't possible for me to have remembered this. She said I must have made it up because babies can't remember anything. She was always correcting me, causing me to forever question what was real. I didn't trust my memories when they contradicted hers. I learned quickly to go along with what she stated as truth.

When I was a child, I didn't understand the dynamic between Debby 1 and Dad, who eloped during spring break of their freshman year in college. Both aged eighteen, they shared the main objective of escaping their parents.

The elopement unfolded during one of Frank and Tracy's carefully curated absences, always to some far-flung corner of the world where they collected photographs like tourist trinkets. I can picture them now: Tracy, beaming beneath a borrowed African headdress with Frank sporting a Chinese farmer's hat with the price tag barely hidden, and both of them flanking bewildered locals with the practiced poses of amateur anthropologists. Their photos graced the next year's Christmas card, evidence of their worldliness carefully arranged between five-star hotel receipts and room service bills for hamburgers and fries.

These were more than just vacations—they were performance art, a master class in selective vision that defined my grandparents' entire existence. They navigated life like tourists in their own reality, choosing which scenes made it into the family album and which ones got cropped out. Their talent for overlooking inconvenient truths rivaled their skill at finding American chain restaurants in foreign capitals: Both were exercises in avoiding anything that might crack their carefully constructed facade of success.

This epitomizes how Frank and Tracy existed—dismissing the reality in front of them in favor of what they *wanted* to see. They overlooked suffering. Ignored anything that did not match the veneer of the successful American life they had created for themselves. They disregarded other people's reality.

Frank and Tracy came home from their trip to find Debby and Don in their bed, their marriage certificate cast aside on the floor.

Debby and Don met in Arlington, Virginia. They were both twelve years old and in the eighth grade. It was Don's first year living in the United States. His parents, Ruth and Don Sr., were stationed overseas when he was born, so Don spent his childhood in Taiwan and Japan. He was accustomed to being pampered and living as a wealthy American with servants. That was no longer the case in America, where his parents' money didn't stretch nearly as far. Debby was also raised by rich parents, whom she grew to detest.

Debby and Don dated on and off throughout high school, taking reprieve from their alcoholic parents—Don by drinking more and Debby by doing everything short of having sex with strangers when she was not with Don.

Their plan to elope was without forethought.

Debby 1, the alter who emerged after their spring break elopement, returned to her liberal arts college in Maine. Don decided not to return to college. He didn't like anyone telling him what to do and felt that college was too cumbersome. He didn't understand why professors wanted him to complete homework assignments that were too simple, and he detested being required to be graded and tested. Both terrified him, even with his tested genius IQ of 186, which Ruth, Don's mother, used to repeatedly establish to anyone who would listen.

Adulthood also terrified Don. He didn't want to be responsible for paying bills or holding down a job. He worked as a planner engineer—self-taught—but was too frightened to take the test to get his engineering license. He was petrified of failing, so he coped by never putting himself into positions where he could fall short.

Don didn't want children, but after six years of marriage, Debby 1 insisted. Debby 1 always wanted four children to love and adore her.

Debby 1 flirted with suicide. It started when Debby was fifteen, slitting her wrists and watching herself bleed. She had these "I am a mistake" and "I need to eliminate this mistake" thoughts in high school. She didn't understand her own feelings or the depth of her shame at the time. Cutting herself was a way to make her pain visible.

Debby returned to this strategy in her first year of college, shortly before she and Don eloped. She wanted to die but didn't know why. She didn't have conscious memories of her sexual abuse at Tracy's hands at this point or of Tracy's cruel words, telling her that she was ugly and inconsequential. The truth was still locked away in the vault of trauma inside Debby. Only later would it become clear that these multiple alters were created—splintered—when she was a baby and grew in number with each abuse throughout childhood and into her teenage years. She simply existed in a fog of self-loathing, believing herself unworthy of life. Don, with his tendency toward physical abuse, became the perfect partner for Debby's dance with death. He validated her self-hatred through violence, creating an environment where splitting into additional personalities in adulthood wasn't just an escape—it was survival.

As I later learned in my work in trauma recovery, this is how generational trauma works: Tracy's abuse of Debby echoed her own abuse by Nina and Saphrona, creating a legacy of mothers who harmed their daughters. But where Tracy wielded control through sexual abuse and emotional manipulation, Debby chose to disappear into herself, fracturing into pieces, while I, her daughter, was left to pick up those pieces and make sense of them.

Everything was an uphill battle with Don. He believed in his heart of hearts that everything was complicated and doomed, that problems could never be fixed, which fueled his depression, which then fueled his alcoholism. Debby 1 called him a "Gloomy Gus," always focusing on things not working out.

When I was a few months old, Debby 1 wanted a bookshelf in their bedroom. She decided on a little nook where it could go. She said to Don, "Why don't you get some bricks and some boards and make me a bookshelf?" He said, "Absolutely not. That's not the way to make a bookshelf, it's got to have a different sort of structure and support, and your way will never work." His reasoning continued with "You can't put a bookshelf there" and "I don't know how to do that."

The reasons for not building the bookshelf continued for weeks.

Debby 1 eventually got some bricks and some boards, making the bookshelf herself in twenty minutes. That bookshelf lasted twelve years, until we moved out of the house.

Decades later, Debby explained to us kids that Don didn't know where to put his anger—a simplistic rationalization that masked a more complex truth. Before I was born, Don flew into rages, looking for a fight, manufacturing conflict as an excuse to disappear into alcohol, just as Debby disappeared into her alters. Debby 1, the alter who tried to maintain some semblance of normalcy, eventually learned to read the warning signs of his impending explosions, but in those early years, she engaged rather than retreated.

Don's fists continued what Tracy's abuse had started, creating the perfect conditions for Debby's mind to continue to splinter. Six years into their marriage and while pregnant with me, Don broke Debby 1's ankle by shoving her. The physical abuse increased after that. Each time he hit her, another crack formed in her psyche, creating another potential doorway for a new alter to emerge. While Debby later told this story through different alters' voices, I understood each was just one perspective among many. Each personality held a different piece of the trauma, each one born from moments like these when reality became too painful to face as a whole person.

Debby 1 was meek, gentle, and achingly loving toward my brothers and me. She existed in only two dimensions: as our devoted mother and as Dad's target for abuse. When Dad's rage needed somewhere to land, Debby 1 absorbed every blow—physical and emotional—as if her body were designed solely to be a buffer between his violence and the rest of us.

When I turned fourteen, my parents finally separated, and something in our family shifted irreversibly. Debby 1—the alter who had absorbed years of violence like a human shield—simply vanished, as if she too had fled with my father. Perhaps she had served her purpose, protecting us through the darkest years. By then, in addition to mothering my brothers, I had assumed the role of caretaker of my parents, managing not just Don's alcoholic absences but also the rotating cast of Debby's personalities, each one carrying a different fragment of our family's shattered story.

CHAPTER FOUR
FIVE AND ALICE

Five and Alice were my most constant childhood companions—two little girls trapped in my mother's mind, each as real to me as the dolls we played with. At five years of age, I didn't know that other mothers didn't dissolve into four- and five-year-old versions of themselves or that my playmates were fragments of my mother's fractured psyche. I only knew that sometimes Mom became my perfect companion, sliding down to my level with an ease that felt like magic.

Five would burst forward with the uncontained energy of a kindergartener, while Alice carried herself with the precious formality of a child mimicking grown-up manners. They emerged from Debby like actors taking their cues, each with their own distinct personality, their own way of inhabiting my mother's adult body.

On one cloudy, cold afternoon, Five appears first. "Let's play!" she announces, her voice lifting with the singsong quality that always signals her arrival.

"Okay, what do you want to play?" I ask, already knowing the answer.

"Dolls!" Five's predictability is comforting—she always starts with dolls, creating an opening for Alice to make her entrance.

Right on cue, Alice's more measured voice emerges: "I'll get the tea set." The ritual begins, as familiar to me as a bedtime story. We gather around my little blue table, its hand-painted flowers marking it as special, different from the hand-me-down furniture in the rest of the house. The white, plastic teacups with their pink flowers stand ready for our make-believe brew, while my Raggedy Ann doll—a gift from my grandmother Ruth—sits patiently in the single matching chair.

Alice approaches teatime with the gravity of a royal butler. "I shall pour the tea," she insists, as she always does. She struggles with Debby's adult body, complaining it's "too big to move," propping up her pouring arm in a gesture I've seen countless times.

The white teapot with its single pink flower wobbled in her grip—a child's mind trying to coordinate adult hands.

The tea service is Alice's domain, her rules as rigid as any Victorian hostess. "Now you can drink your tea," she instructs, adding with maternal authority, "Make sure Raggedy Ann drinks some too."

The other cups await Five's and Alice's turns, though Five's restlessness already crackles through Debby's body. "Let's play with crayons!" she bursts out, the suggestion landing more like a declaration.

In the space of a heartbeat, Alice returns for her final bow, meticulously putting away the tea set with prim satisfaction. Then Five resurfaces, rummaging through my room with the single-minded determination of a child on a treasure hunt. I watch these transitions with the expertise of a tiny anthropologist—I've learned to track Five's boundless enthusiasm against Alice's measured propriety, each personality as distinct as fingerprints on my childhood.

These moments felt normal to me then—just another afternoon with my mother's youngest selves, each one offering a different flavor of the childhood companionship I craved. It was years before I understood that most mothers don't fragment, that tea parties aren't usually hosted by alternate personalities taking turns in the same body, and that Debby had something called alternate personalities.

Later, when I was older and Debby was finally diagnosed, I learned Five's and Alice's names. I asked them to go back Inside (into the recesses of Debby's mind) when I needed Debby to sign my field trip slip or drive the car. Five and Alice both knew how to drive, but I never thought it was a good idea to have a child behind the wheel.

They were fascinated by the big-girl body they inhabited and thought it was fun to be able to see so easily over the steering wheel and do grown-up things. Neither of them could read, so I'm not sure exactly how they negotiated with street and road signs. I just assume now that other alters helped them out with that.

All of Debby's clothes looked gigantic on them, and her shoes were too big for them. They liked playing dress-up with her makeup and thought it was funny when other people (outside of our family) spoke to them like they were grown-ups.

Five was extremely imaginative and liked it when I played make-believe with her. Once I became a teenager, she told me that I "got boring" and she didn't want to play with me anymore.

My younger brothers liked that Five did things like melted crayons on foil directly on top of the burners on our electric stove to create foil art and somehow knew how to combine vinegar, dish soap, and baking soda to make things explode. Alice was more ladylike than Five, and kept her play to dolls and tea parties.

Five and Alice, like most of the alters, were one-dimensional. They both liked to play, and when playtime was over, they disappeared.

I believe that Five and Alice were the alters that emerged to protect Debby when George, her paternal grandfather, watched her in vulnerable moments. These alters took over when she was naked in the bath her grandmother Nana drew for her, or while changing clothes in the bedroom. Each alter served as a shield, a way to fragment the experience into something survivable.

Later, through various alters, Debby simply described George, whom she called Pappy, as "voyeuristic." "He wasn't that bad," she said, "because he would only ever watch—he never touched us." The plural "us" wasn't just a slip—it was a glimpse into how her mind had already begun to splinter, creating multiple selves to endure the violation of his gaze. I guess, compared to Tracy's sexual abuse of her, her grandfather's prying eyes seemed mild—another example of how horror becomes relative when trauma is the baseline.

This warped hierarchy of abuse—ranking violations from "mild" to severe—helped explain why Debby's psyche needed so many different personalities to process her childhood. Each alter held a different shade of trauma: Five and Alice for grandfather George's voyeurism, others for Tracy's more direct abuse, still others for the everyday task of pretending everything was normal. It was a complex system of survival.

CHAPTER FIVE

TEN

The alter Ten was a demon monster—not a metaphor but a literal manifestation of rage in human form.

I am six or seven years old when I first meet Ten, an age when most children are learning to trust their parents as safe harbors. It is late afternoon, that liminal space between homework and dinner when the day's light begins to fade. I have done something that triggered Debby's switch, and Ten appears out of nowhere, like a horror movie monster materializing in our mundane reality. Ten is pure anger incarnate and terrifies me with an otherworldly presence. It begins chasing me through our tiny house—living room, dining room, kitchen, hallway—each space becoming part of a nightmare maze. I know, with the bone-deep certainty of a child, that I am going to be killed.

I didn't understand why my mother wanted to kill me. This confusion—the disconnect between the mother who sometimes loved me and this demon who wanted to destroy me—later helped me understand how Debby could fragment into pieces.

Running into my bedroom, I slam the door shut, lock it, and climb onto the top of my bunk bed, hiding under covers that offer no real protection. Ten pounds on the door with inhuman force, making it shudder in its frame, screaming, "Let me in! Let me in! Let me in!" Its screams echo through the house like a twisted fairy tale, the Big Bad Wolf wearing my mother's face. My father isn't around, most likely having already retreated to the basement to drink as soon as he came home from work.

Too terrified to move, I don't leave my room until the next morning, enduring hunger and a full bladder rather than risking another encounter. I stare at my wall, at a poster of a white tiger I found in a National Geographic that brings me comfort. It is my imaginary friend when I am lonely and scared.

This night became my first lesson in surviving Debby's multiplicity—that safety sometimes meant choosing the lesser discomfort. I know now that parents can experience anger toward their children, many even have moments of metaphorically murderous thoughts. Parents might pound on doors in frustration, seeking resolution. But most parents remain whole people, capable of processing a full spectrum of emotions and finding their way back to rationality.

Ten was not capable of this. First of all, Ten wasn't a parent— Ten was, as you might guess, ten years old, frozen in prepubescent rage. Ten wasn't even male or female; Ten was only ever anger, pure and unfiltered. This alter's eyes were yellow, with vertical pupils like a dragon, a detail that would sound fantastical if I hadn't seen them myself countless times. I felt evil and hatred radiating from Ten like heat from a furnace.

When the other alters experienced fear, Ten was the one who emerged to manage the situation through uncontrolled rage. There was no rationalizing or coaxing with Ten, only waves of violence. Subconsciously, after that event, one of my life goals became making sure Ten never came Out again. I became my own protector and the protector of my siblings.

Nearly a decade later, after Dad moved out, the upstairs bathroom toilet began leaking. Water seeped out in a steady flow, eroding the caulk between the two-inch-by-two-inch pink bathroom floor tiles, and rotting the wood floorboards below. Debby called a handyman to remove the toilet, replace the rotting wood floor, and retile around the toilet. The handyman and his helper arrived early on a Wednesday afternoon. Debby was at work so she couldn't be there. I left high school early to let them in.

The project was bigger than originally thought. It took hours for the two men to remove the toilet and load it in their truck, remove the tile and floorboards, and replace the wood.

It was 7:00 p.m. by the time the last nail was in the wood floor. Debby was home from work, and we had already eaten dinner. She was becoming increasingly agitated by the men walking up and down the stairs next to the living room and coming in and out of the house.

Debby's eyes closed, and a moment later Ten was in her place, screaming at the men: "Get out! Get out! Get out!" This was always how it went. One alter was Out, and we were in the middle of an activity, or a conversation, or something, then Debby's eyes closed and in less than thirty seconds, her eyes opened and a different alter came Out.

I had trained myself to anticipate this switching of personalities. I watched her physically and knew when something was going to happen much more easily than by anticipating the switch using context. Everything triggered Debby, so context wasn't a helpful reference point. But her physical body was.

I was always on high alert when Debby was present. It was exhausting to stand at attention, anticipating danger or sadness or fear, or, with Ten, rage, to anticipate the switch, to manage the switch, and to manage myself.

The screaming continued. The plumber and his helper looked confused. I was confused. They were so close to being done with the job, and they had been incredibly polite the entire time. They were skipping their opportunity to be home, to be having dinner with their families, and were instead working late at our house so they wouldn't have to come back the next day, and Ten was raging at them.

I apologized profusely to the men, grabbed Debby's checkbook out of her purse, and wrote them a check for services rendered. Although I was terrified of Ten with its slit yellow eyes, I looked it in the eye and said that I would take care of everything—*I will install the new toilet, now sitting upstairs in the hallway, and retile the floor.*

Of course, I had no idea how to do either of these things.

Ten sits down in Debby's chair in the living room. Eyes close, and out pops Five, always eager to play. "Let's play!" she announces, excited and eager to be Out.

"Five, I can't play with you right now. I'm busy. I need you to go find Alex or Edward. They will play with you."

She runs off down the hallway in search of them. Five is mainly harmless, especially because I had a long talk with her about how she's not allowed to go near the stove anymore to melt crayons without my supervision.

I assess the risk of leaving versus staying at home with Alex, Edward, and Five, and decide to leave. Technically, there is someone in an adult body in the house. It's virtually impossible for me to summon another alter to show up on demand. I've tried before, unsuccessfully, like when Five or Alice show up when Debby is driving the car.

I yell down the hallway to Alex, "I have to go get something. I'll be home in one hour. Lock the door behind me."

I recently got my driver's license, so I grab Debby's car keys and drive to the public library, hoping I can get in before they close at 8:00 p.m. I do and ask the researcher in the adult section to help me find books on how to install a toilet and floor tile.

This was before the internet and personal computers.

That night, I'm up until midnight, reading through the two books I checked out from the library and making a list of supplies I need to get at the hardware store the next day to complete the job.

This is how I managed most of the alters. I decided I would be the parent and adult they were not capable of being.

CHAPTER SIX
DEBBIE

In my very early childhood, Debbie emerges as a whirlwind of creative energy, a force of nature designed to fill the void left by our father's emotional absence. She doesn't just compensate—she overcompensates with the determination of a one-woman theatrical troupe. Where he retreats, she advances; where he dims, she blazes.

Debbie is perpetual motion personified, transforming every moment into an opportunity for growth and discovery. She orchestrates our days like a master conductor: turning breakfast into impromptu science experiments, morphing mundane car rides into history lessons, and spinning ordinary afternoons into peace rallies where we make protest signs with glitter and hope. Her creativity isn't just artistic—it's survival artistry, crafting a world where education and activism dance together in our living room.

Debbie wears her extroversion like a suit of armor, polished to a shine that almost blinds you to the wounds it protects. Every volunteer committee, every PTA meeting, every community project becomes another stage for her performance of perfect motherhood. She doesn't just participate—she orchestrates, organizes, revolutionizes. It's as if she's racing against time, trying to pack a lifetime of mothering into whatever moments she can claim from the chaos of multiple personalities.

If Debbie were a color, she'd be electric blue—bright, impossible to ignore, and slightly overwhelming. If she were music, she'd be a marching band playing at double time. But she's not just activities for activities' sake; she's a desperate assertion of presence, a way of saying,

"Look, I'm here, I'm mothering, I'm making it count." Every craft project, every educational game, and every peace march is her way of leaving fingerprints on my childhood, evidence that someone was trying their hardest to mother through the fractures.

I don't know when or how this alter was formed. She was frequently present in my youth. When I was three years old, I was standing with Debbie outside the largest hotel in Washington, DC, just down the road from the National Zoo. We were occupying the street corner.

We are protesting a nuclear arms convention at the Marriott Hotel. I am holding Debbie's hand with my left hand and a protest sign with my right. I am watching other mothers with their children walk past us up the long hill to the National Zoo. I keep asking Debbie when we can go to the zoo.

She says, "Not now, we're changing the world." I don't know what this means exactly, only that we are surrounded by other people who are chanting and raising their arms in protest to the men in suits walking out of the hotel. The mothers and children walking past stare at us as if we are alien creatures. Changing the world doesn't seem very fun to me.

Debbie plants seeds of possibility in my young mind with the fervor of a spiritual gardener tending sacred soil. She doesn't just teach—she weaves a tapestry of belief so vibrant that, in her presence, the world transforms into a canvas of unlimited potential. Her voice, warm and certain, paints pictures of a future where my dreams aren't just personal treasures but tools for global transformation.

"You can change the world," she tells me, not as a cliché but as an article of faith, a mandate passed down with the weight of holy scripture. In her gospel of social responsibility, education isn't merely a path to personal success—it's a torch we carry to light the way for others. She instills in me the belief that knowledge, like love, multiplies when shared, and that true learning must ripple outward into action.

Her definition of goodness is both beautiful and burning: Good people give until they're empty, then find more to give. She crafts this message into every bedtime story, every homework session, every volunteer project she drags me to. Through her lens, selflessness isn't just a virtue—it's the highest form of existence, the gold standard against which all actions should be measured.

Looking back, I see how she was sculpting more than just my character; she was crafting a spiritual warrior, a future champion for change. Her teachings were both gift and burden: the exhilarating freedom to dream without limits, tethered to the weighty responsibility of serving others.

Debbie raised me to believe that God is in every person. I learned that the homeless men, women, and children we volunteered to feed weekly in shelters and soup kitchens have the same needs, desires, and dreams as I did, and that loving them is akin to loving myself.

Debbie also taught me that my needs were inappropriate in our family and that I must be a "good little girl" and behave the way she expected me to at all times.

"Stop crying."

"Stop coughing, you're making too much noise."

"Can't you see that I'm doing something else right now?"

My role as Debbie's companion at these events partly stemmed from our unconventional education arrangement. Traditional schooling and I had a brief, uncomfortable courtship—I entered first grade at five, bypassing Montessori entirely, only to find myself bewildered by the rigid choreography of public education. The endless lines, the arbitrary rules, the emphasis on compliance over curiosity—it all felt like an elaborate performance with no clear purpose. By fifth grade, I had developed enough self-awareness and courage to voice what I'd known intuitively all along: My mind didn't fit into their prescribed boxes of learning. The same independence that helped me navigate our chaotic home life made me resistant to the lock-step rhythm of traditional education. A few weeks into fifth grade I announced that I could not learn in the way my teachers expected me to learn, and I refused to return to school.

In a rare moment of maternal clarity, Debbie supported my pronouncement. It was one of those moments where her extroverted activism aligned perfectly with my needs, and she made a decision that reshaped our family's trajectory: She pulled both Bryce and me out of elementary school.

We are the first family in our county to legally homeschool. Debbie negotiates with the school superintendent and barters with her friends to teach me German and Italian. She collaborates with the county to establish metrics for evaluating our learning so we can stay competitive with our peers.

Homeschooling is perfect for me. Textbook learning, which previously occupied eight hours of a school day, is now compressed into an hour and a half in the mornings, followed by explorations and learning on topics I find interesting for the rest of the day.

Debbie is freelancing for a local newspaper, writing articles about activities parents can do with their children. We continually explore places for her to write about in and around DC. As a result, most homeschooling for Bryce and me is hands-on learning.

I flourish in this environment. I love being independent and in charge of my own learning experience. I want to learn. I want to expand my horizons. I'm always up for new adventures.

Bryce, however, retreats into himself. He was already a loner in school, and homeschooling is making him even more lonely. I watch his external personality disappear. He is almost always stuck inside himself. Gazing out into nothing, his mouth gaping open, he creates worlds of adventure inside the recesses of his mind. Every time I try to talk to him, it takes him minutes to recognize I am speaking to him and that I expect a response from him. I don't know how to be friends with someone who doesn't exist.

We didn't yet know that Bryce had been sexually abused by Tracy and by one of the boys in our neighborhood, who was my age. We didn't yet know that Bryce would become the target for so much of Dad's rage. Bryce's solution to living in a violent world was to disassociate from it, just like Debby modeled for us.

My childhood friends loved to join us for planned excursions. Debbie often interviewed my friends for their take on family activities in and around DC. They went with us to explore, like to the Orkin

Insect Zoo at the National Museum of Natural History, where we got to see tarantulas up close! Or to the Capital Children's Museum with exhibits we could touch, or to the Enchanted Forest in Maryland, where fairy tales came alive in playground form.

Debbie normalized the years of Saturday mornings we spent at a soup kitchen, flipping pancakes at 6:00 a.m. for 300 homeless men, and the Wednesday afternoons spent at a women's shelter, preparing sandwiches for homeless children. Christmas Day was spent delivering gifts to homeless men, women, and children on the streets of Washington, DC.

We rode the bus whenever possible. Our clothes were donated to area shelters, and we shopped at thrift stores because we didn't have the money, but also because Debbie simply did not believe in consumerism. Friday mornings, once a month, were spent in a friend's garage, where a neighborhood co-op distributed bulk foods to our family and others. Debbie bartered for my piano lessons by making dinner once a week for my piano teacher's family.

With Debbie, we always had adventures, in our yard, in our community, in our region. We were on the go, and I loved our life during the day. As long as we went along with Debbie's agenda, everything was okay. I learned quickly to always say yes and thrive within this agenda. I was a good captive.

When we were very young, we were members of the Christian Science Church. Tracy had occasionally taken Debby to worship with Christian Scientists. Debbie seemed to find their theology comforting. Christian Scientists view Jesus as the Son of God, not as fully Divine, demonstrating divinity as God's child.

Christian Scientists embrace a radical interpretation of healing that challenges conventional medical wisdom. Their doctrine, established by Mary Baker Eddy in the late 19th century, posits that illness exists primarily in thought rather than physical reality. They view disease as a manifestation of incorrect thinking requiring spiritual correction through prayer as the primary pathway to healing.

I found certain aspects appealing. The religion being founded by a woman was cool to me. Mary Baker Eddy believed women had the right to be as enlightened and empowered as men in the late 19th century. She demanded an entirely new world be created for both sexes, where all people exist in the image and likeness of God, who is Spirit.

When I was little, women ministered from the pulpit as First or Second Readers. I learned that women could hold authority. This planted the idea that I could be a woman minister with my own authority. In my family, I wasn't allowed my own voice. This religion gave me another way to see myself.

Christian Science was also isolating and punishing. If I was sick, I was told to pray better because ineffective prayer caused disease in my body. I was taught that when my body hurts, something is wrong with my state of mind and my belief in God.

All four of us were born at home with a midwife and never vaccinated or taken to doctors.

I was taught that being in my body is dangerous.

When I have symptoms, Debbie dismisses them: "Stop coughing, you're making too much noise." "Stop pretending you are sick." "You're not sick." "Stop making yourself the center of attention."

My perpetual strep throat goes untreated until college. When I need dental care, it is my responsibility to earn the money to pay for a cavity filling, book the appointment, and get myself to the dentist's office.

I detest getting sick, knowing it will only result in punishment. I learn to make myself numb, shut my body down, keep my voice steady, and not move too much lest I be noticed.

The result was severe emotional and sexual repression throughout adolescence. I hid to survive. I never dated in junior high or high school, didn't kiss a boy until college, and shied away from conversations about sex.

One Sunday morning when I was twelve, I found a homeless man in our church's stairwell. As I offered him help, my Sunday School teacher yanked me back inside, announcing, "We don't interact with people like that." I told Debbie I refused to return to this unwell-coming church. We negotiated to attend Quaker Meeting instead.

This was a rare moment when I confronted Debbie and she sided with me, because I had advocated for someone else rather than myself.

We had been active with Quakers for years through volunteer work. Initially, Quakerism exists for us in soup kitchens, protests, and at the White House fence where Debbie takes us when she feels the world is broken.

We are always surrounded by Quakers in these places, awkwardly dressed in hand-me-downs from Goodwill, crowds sprinkled with older women whose braided hair is pinned into large buns at the nape of their necks.

Quakerism teaches me that God is in every person, including me. I am special and capable as God's child. I can hear God's voice as clearly as any adult. It feels good not to have an intermediary.

Debbie—the playful, extroverted alter who served as our primary mother figure—disappeared within a year of Tracy's death. The personality who filled our days with activities and laughter, creating a facade of normalcy, simply vanished. Gone were the moments of manufactured joy that helped us pretend we were just another family.

Debbie was the first of several alters to disappear over the years, each fading once their protective purpose was fulfilled. Her role was clear: the smokescreen who kept us distracted from the horrors around us—the abuse Debby endured from Dad, our violations at his and Tracy's hands. She created pockets of childhood normalcy while other alters carried trauma's weight.

Debbie's disappearance marked a shift in our family's emotional landscape. Without Debbie's orchestrated distractions, reality became harder to ignore. The stage manager of our family's performance had quit, leaving harsh lights to illuminate every crack in our backdrop. This pushed me further into mothering my brothers, filling the void left by all the parts of our mother that would continue disappearing, one personality at a time.

FAMILY SECRETS
(1987–1990)

CHAPTER SEVEN

24

Our family structure began its steady decline on March 8, 1987, the day Tracy died.

Tracy's death sparked a revolution inside Debby, and the infantry spilled Out through the revolving door that is her body.

The alters began showing up so fast and furiously that we were unable to keep track of them all. Some were catatonic, others, infants. Others engaged but refused to share their names or identify themselves.

None of us knew what they were yet. We just knew there was something very, very wrong with Debby.

After Tracy's death, Debby becomes severely depressed. I never recall her caring for my youngest brother, Edward, only ten months old when Tracy dies. Over and over, I find Debby upstairs, lying alone in my parents' bed in the darkness, curtains closed, quiet and still.

Debby's seat at the dinner table is perpetually empty. My father often physically drags her out of their bedroom to come and eat with us, sometimes by her arms, other times by her hair.

"Get in the chair! Debby, get in the chair now, and eat your dinner!" His rage masks his fear. Dad has no idea how to cope when Debby is nonfunctional.

We watch this happen, obediently sitting in our chairs in the dining room, night after night. I am terrified of our father when he gets like this. When he goes after the boys, I feel like I can fight back, but not when he goes after Debby. Something inside of me keeps me glued to my chair and mute.

The alter 24 sits in Debby's seat, her head hung low, moving the food on her plate around with a fork, until the rest of us finish eating, then returns to bed.

24 came to life when Debby was twenty-four, the year I was born. She balanced out Debby 1's desire to live and raise children with her own steadfast commitment to death. I don't remember how I learned the name of this personality. Another alter must have told me.

I believe that when Debby became a mother, some unconscious part of her recognized the perils of motherhood, as exhibited by Tracy, and thought her death was the only solution for not destroying her own children.

Thus the creation of 24.

On a Saturday morning, about six months after Tracy's death, I discover 24 in the upstairs bathroom, wrists slit crossways, calmly waiting for the blood to leave her body. Razor blades, the ones my father uses for shaving, are in the sink, which is filled with blood. (Later I learned that slitting wrists crosswise instead of lengthwise is generally a cry for attention, not a serious attempt at death.)

The bathroom has a sink, toilet, bathtub, and floor tile, all in mismatched shades of pink. The red blood against them makes the room radiate.

It is early fall, unseasonably warm, and I have plans to go for a long bike ride that day, taking the paved bike path at the end of our street that runs alongside Highway 66, straight into Washington, DC. My plan is to take the path all the way to the Key Bridge, which crosses over into DC, then turn around and bike home. This trip will take me several hours. I have already packed snacks and two water bottles in my fanny pack.

My blue ten-speed bike is my pride and joy. Riding it keeps me from hovering around the house all day, waiting for the inevitable shit to hit the proverbial fan. Long, solitary hours on the bike paths around DC are my salvation during these years with my family. Because it's the 1980s, no one can contact me when I am riding. I am free and alone.

At the end of my ride, I find 24. Her body is motionless, as if she is willing it to stop breathing. She won't respond to my asking her what is wrong. She is lifeless, devoid of emotion.

I call out to my father, who eventually, reluctantly, comes up from the basement. His emotions cycle quickly from concern, to irritation, to loud anger. Together we move 24's body down the stairs, situating her in a seated position on the bottom step, directly in sight of the front door. My father wraps her wrists in old T-shirts, then looks at me and bellows, "You are in charge. Take care of your brothers. Don't let your mother fall asleep or go back upstairs." Then he leaves.

I take charge for the remainder of that day. I know what is expected of me. I make dinner. I hold baby Edward when he cries. At least six loads of laundry get cleaned, folded, and put away. I help Bryce with his science homework. But for the most part, my focus is on ensuring 24 doesn't fall asleep, mainly because I don't want Dad to be mad when he gets home.

Dad always came home. He preferred to drink in the privacy of our basement rather than out at a bar. But I have no memory of him coming home that night.

I have no recollection of him caring for Debby following this first suicide attempt. Sometime later, 24 told me that Dad would physically kick her out of their bed and make her sleep on the floor if she showed too many emotions.

It's easy to imagine this might have been his response to her suicide attempt as well.

There are blank spaces in my memories, places I can't recollect because part of me needs to believe my parents didn't make the choices they often made when we were in crisis. Dad leaving our suicidal mother alone with four young children at home is one of those choices.

We didn't take Debby to the hospital the day she slit her wrists. What I do know is that Debby didn't get the help she needed then, and her pattern of wanting to die actively continued for a decade.

CHAPTER EIGHT
DAD

I don't remember observing my parents enjoying each other's company, or the sound of my father's laugh, or his interest in any aspect of my life, with one exception.

I was homeschooled during fifth and sixth grade, primarily by Debbie. During this time, Debbie traveled to Germany to research an article she was writing. She asked my father to take time off from work to homeschool me and Bryce while she was gone. My father deeply considered the most important thing he could impart to his eldest child and decided to teach me everything he knew about classical music.

For two weeks straight, we transformed the dining room walls into a giant timeline, listing the dates of birth and death for all major composers, noting their most famous compositions and key events in their lives. We listened to every record my father owned. We discussed the various instruments and the distinction between a sonata and a minuet. I learned the progression of symphonies, the logic behind the language choices in major choral works, and the radical forms of chord progressions and use of instrumentation.

I discovered how different pieces and instruments made me feel. Turned out I was not a fan of the harpsichord, but I loved the way Bach used it in *The Goldberg Variations*, considered the most serious and ambitious composition written for this instrument. In it, the harpsichord is demure, invitational, and welcoming instead of demanding its seat at the table, like I had heard in so many of his other works.

We listen to Mahler's Sixth Symphony, which is brutal, seemingly never-ending, and without relief. The hammer strikes, signaling a mighty blow of fate, and Dad is visibly moved. My father loves this piece, and I don't know why. He doesn't exhibit the courage or the impulse to find fulfillment in his life, which is Mahler's essential message in this symphony.

The Lacrimosa movement of Mozart's final Requiem, the Requiem in D Minor, stirs both of us with its power. Years later, I sing this piece in a choral performance, lending my voice to guilty men being judged, and spared.

"Für Elise," published after Beethoven's death, is a sweet love song, which I later learned to play on the piano, flowing arpeggios between my left and right hands, discovering how to keep the time signature of 3/8 for the main section.

I developed opinions about each of Vivaldi's *The Four Seasons* movements: Winter (like it), Spring (boring), Summer (nope), and Fall (my favorite).

At ten years old, I found all of this a bit overwhelming but cool. Dad was thrilled to share his love of classical music with me. I have forgotten a lot of what he taught me, but my appreciation of classical music has carried with me throughout my life. It's been a comfort and a mainstay, a language that exists for me in the spiritual realms.

Much of my life I convinced myself and others that my father had little to no impact on me. The truth is he gave me love of music and creative expression, which helped me to launch my initial career in the arts.

I joined a choral group in college. After college, I worked for one of the top three choral groups in DC and sang with them as well. At twenty-four, I launched my own arts consulting firm, working with arts organizations to help them secure corporate sponsorship and events. I met Yo-Yo Ma, Itzhak Perlman, Joshua Bell, Emanuel Ax, and Andre Watts in person. I attended live performances by orchestras from around the world.

This one solid positive memory with my father I hold on to, because once Tracy died, Dad's violence got out of control.

———————

After Tracy dies in the spring of 1987, Dad is dealing with a very depressed wife, a toddler, and three other young children. We had moved into a bigger house in 1986, and I can imagine he is feeling the weight of all the new financial responsibility. His drinking steadily increases, as does his isolation.

When not at work, he spends all of his time in our basement, not participating in family life.

One Friday night in the first year after Tracy dies, Debbie—the volunteer alter—is out of the house. Remarkably, even in the midst of Debby's depression and the chaos of her personalities cycling through our home, Debbie maintains her commitment to helping strangers. She is constantly finding new causes to join, as if saving others might somehow compensate for the damage being done at home. Her latest interest is prostitutes in Washington, DC, who need medical care—another group of vulnerable women, perhaps reflecting parts of herself she can't yet face.

Debbie goes out on Friday nights with a local pastor and other volunteers, roaming the streets where prostitutes conduct their business. This area transforms from a bustling business district during the day into a well-known prostitution corner after sunset—a duality that mirrors Debby's own split existence. She volunteers medical support and talks with them about safe sex practices, while back home, I'm left managing my three younger brothers' safety and basic needs.

It is early spring 1988, one of those days when it's warm enough during the day to wear a T-shirt and shorts but cold enough at night for frost to accumulate on the grass. I am fourteen and in the kitchen getting a snack, when I hear a commotion in the basement. Dad is down there, of course, drinking whiskey and watching the news. For some reason, Bryce is also in the basement, along with two-year-old Edward, who is playing on a blanket on the floor.

Dad is screaming and beating on Bryce. Dad is strong. He's only five feet, eight inches but nearly 350 pounds, and he can throw a punch. He has Bryce, who at eleven is almost as tall as he is, pinned up against a wall. The basement wall acts as a buttress, a silent conspirator in holding Bryce up, so Dad can continue to hit him. I have no idea what has upset Dad because Bryce is introverted and meek and never looks for a fight. Edward is wailing. Six-year-old Alex is upstairs in his room.

I run down the basement stairs. With less than a minute to assess the situation before I become our father's next target, I pick up Edward and rush upstairs with him while Dad is still hitting Bryce. In my haste, I carry Edward awkwardly, and his head bangs against the stairwell wall, exacerbating his screams. I know I can't save all three of my brothers. I figure I have the best chance to grab Alex too since he's already safely upstairs.

I take Edward and Alex. We sneak out the back door of the house, climb over the chain link fence between our house and our neighbors, and silently walk through the neighbor's yard, across the street, and into the neighborhood park.

It is almost dark, still bright enough to see shapes and shadows but dim enough not to be easily spotted. We hide behind the bleachers in the baseball field. This is an excellent spot, because I can see the road closest to our house as well as the road that Debby will drive home on. It is also a great vantage point to see our father if he walks into the park.

Twenty minutes or so later, I see Bryce running into the park. He somehow knew that we left to hide here, or perhaps by then our father has figured out that we were no longer in the house. I call to him, and he camouflages himself with us. I hug him and look him over for bruises. We don't talk about his being hit. We are too scared of our father finding all four of us to talk at all. It's cold, but we're all in shorts and T-shirts. I am trying to keep Edward warm enough so he won't cry.

We see our father drive to the park and stop the car in the parking lot. He gets out and screams at us to come home. We remain silent and hidden behind the bleachers.

I am terrified. I shield my brothers from my terror by pretending I know what to do next. I tell them to stay quiet and that Dad will leave soon.

Dad eventually gets back in the car and drives past the park, toward the neighborhood shops, most likely his next stop to try and find us. I imagine he won't be gone for more than twenty minutes. By then we are shivering and need to get someplace warmer. Gathering my brothers, I tell them we are going to run back into the house and lock the doors before our father comes home. I use my most authoritative voice.

When we get back to the house, I tell Bryce to lock the kitchen door, the back door, and the basement door. I tell Alex that he's going to be okay and to go up to his room and get into bed. I follow him to put Edward to bed in the room he shares with Alex. In my haste to get everyone back into the house I forget to lock the front door all the way. Only the lock on the door handle has been turned. The chain lock and deadbolt are still undone. My terror has seeped its way into my ability to use my brain.

Our father comes home a few minutes later in a rage, pounding on the front door, demanding that we let him in. We never lock the doors, except at night when we are sleeping. I glance over and see his house keys on the kitchen counter. My hands are shaking as I lock the deadbolt, but I can't turn it all the way because the door is vibrating too much. I do get the chain link secured. Walking the eight feet from the front door to the kitchen, I pick up the phone on the wall to call the police.

Just then my father breaks the handle on the front door, and all that remains between him and our living room is the chain lock, hanging precariously by one screw. I can see his face as he's trying to get inside the house and screaming at me. I am holding the phone in my hand, but I can't remember the three numbers—911—I need to press to contact the police. I push nine and freeze.

Then my mind goes blank. The last thing I remember is staring at the keypad and hearing my father yelling. I don't remember if my father gets back inside the house. I have no recollection of police coming to the house or of Debby arriving home.

I do remember having a conversation with Debby the next day. "Look, Mom, look what Dad did to the front door. It's not safe in the house with him. You need to protect us. You have to kick him out." I show her the damage to the front door, and I explain to her that she needs to choose between her husband and her children, because she can't have both.

I'm unsure which of the alters I had that conversation with, because at that time we still didn't know that Debby definitely had alternate personalities.

I have no idea what I will do with my brothers and myself if Debby chooses our father instead of us, but I know it is ultimatum time. I genuinely believe she is going to pick Dad, so I am vaguely thinking about calling Debby's sister to see if she has any ideas for where we can go. She lives many hours away from us, and we see her infrequently, but she is always levelheaded and reasonable.

I decide to deliver the ultimatum and then go pack up clothes for the boys and me so we can make a quick getaway if needed. I imagine Debby will tell Dad about the ultimatum and he will respond with violence, as usual. Remarkably, Debby tells our father he needs to move out, and he does, within a few months.

Nearly forty years later, I asked Debby about this night.

She wrote, "I vaguely remember coming home from volunteering with Exodus Youth Services (which helped street kids) and finding your father alone, saying you all had run out. I told him we had to go find you and started walking toward the park—and right past you, I think. One of you told me that. Was it Alex? You eventually came home, thank God. I don't remember your telling me about the incident, though it makes sense you would have; what I do remember is Alex asking for a bodyguard. Up to that point, I thought Don only hit me, and I hadn't seen him hit you kids. When I heard this, I got a lawyer and started divorce proceedings."

My recalling Debbie volunteering with prostitutes is replaced with her stating that she was helping street kids, which of course sounds more appropriate for a mother to be doing.

Dad's breaking down the front door and my attempting to call 911 is replaced with Debbie coming home hours earlier than normal and immediately searching for us. My telling Debby she has to choose between us and Dad is replaced with her proactively finding a lawyer.

In Debby's rewrite she positions herself as the perfect mother and Good Samaritan.

Which memory do I believe, hers or mine?

Memory is a funny thing. Our memories can be different from other peoples' based on how we consolidate them and our individuated brain differences. Sometimes we create narratives the way we want them to happen. Sometimes we have flashbacks—images or words will come to us—that give us different but incomplete stories.

Identity is built on accounts we create from our past experiences, and these descriptions change over time. That is the normal human experience. But traumatic memories differ from regular memories.

In *The Body Keeps the Score*, Dr. Bessel van der Kolk shares a study of veterans from World War II. Researchers interviewed these veterans every couple of years for forty-five years, asking them about their experiences during the war.

For the veterans who did not develop PTSD, their accounts and their memories changed over time. The events lost the detailed physical sensations and intensity of painful emotions, and the storytelling is softened.

However, the experiences were different for the men who developed PTSD. They may not have remembered all of the details, but the things they did remember remained clear and consistent for over forty-five years after the war had ended. Their traumatic memories were much more vivid than regular memories, and their accounts did not change over the decades.

When traumatic memories are retrieved, the physical stress response actually serves to strengthen them, reinforcing the memory in the brain's circuits. The PTSD response makes these memories more vivid and intense over time.

This is the brain's way of keeping us safe. It has a built-in response to reinforce these traumatic memories, so people won't forget them and will avoid similar situations in the future.

When I recollect that fall night, I remember in grave detail the following:

Edward's wailing and my carrying him up the basement steps, his head hitting the wall because he is using his whole body to scream.

The smell of the grass as we kneel in the park behind the bleachers in the baseball field.

The sound of Dad's hatchback station wagon driving past.

The crack of the doorframe breaking as the locking mechanism is jolted out of position.

The buttons on the phone beeping as I desperately try to remember the numbers for 911.

I smelled and heard these things, and as I remember them, I again, immediately feel unsafe.

Thirty-five years after this incident, Alex brought it up to me out of the blue. He was six when it happened, but his memory is identical to mine. Debby was not home. We hid in the park. Dad was screaming and breaking down the door. Bryce was pinned up against a wall and beaten. What Alex remembers most is that I was there, protecting him, protecting all my brothers. He thanked me for being his protector.

Memory is never given back to us as if we are neutral observers. We each have our own lens through which we see the world. I weigh my memories of that night against Debby's habit of creating new narratives out of thin air to suit her and her circumstances. Which of our experiences actually happened?

Was I living in her delusional world, or she in mine?

This was my daily practice throughout childhood: to sort through Debby's narratives versus mine, forever searching for what was real.

CHAPTER NINE
BRYCE

Looking back, it seems like Bryce had no other choice for coping with our family dysfunction than addiction. It was the only way he could find out of the pain.

I discovered Bryce the first time he overdosed. It was 1989, and he was twelve. It was a school day just before summer break. At my own request, I had entered an alternative public school beginning in seventh grade. Bryce followed my lead and did the same. It had been a good school year for me, and I was excited to see my friends and enjoy my tenth-grade end-of-year activities. School was always a guaranteed safe place for me.

The morning I found Bryce, Debby had already left for work, taking Edward with her to drop him off at daycare. Alex had already left for the bus stop. He was in the first grade at an alternative elementary school on the other side of the county. Our father had moved out six months earlier. It's interesting how easily it all comes back.

Knocking on Bryce's bedroom, I can hear him inside, making weird noises. Opening the door reveals him naked, lying on his back on the wood floor, using his feet to move his body around in circles. He is moaning, perhaps trying to talk, but no coherent words are coming out.

"Bryce, you need to get up."

"Bryce, it's time to go to school."

Then, finally, panicking, my voice catching in my throat, "Bryce, what is wrong with you?"

Bryce will not respond to anything I say to him. I am embarrassed that he is naked. I'm irritated that I have to deal with this. I'm scared that something is really wrong with him.

Terrified, I called Debby at work, and she told me she would come home immediately. She didn't suggest I call 911. Debby must have been the one to track down our father, because I remember him being at the hospital later that day. She and I got Bryce into the car and took him to the emergency room. There, Bryce's stomach is pumped, leaving the outside of his mouth smeared with charcoal.

Since the incident when Dad broke down our front door, our parents' communication had been stiff and full of anger. But this day, things were different. For once, my parents were in complete agreement about how to handle this family situation. They announced it was my job to monitor Bryce to make sure he didn't overdose again.

No one suggested that maybe Bryce needed therapy or that there was something catastrophically wrong in our household that would cause Bryce to overdose. Debby and Don simply gave Bryce a stern talking to about how drugs are bad, thinking that would fix things.

I followed my parents' lead, that Bryce's overdose was a slight nuisance, like a fly to keep swatting away, but nothing that would cause any harm. Except it did cause harm. Bryce was already lost to us by the time he was twelve. All sense of him as an innocent young boy was gone. His drug use immediately became a full-blown addiction that never ended.

I will always regret that Friday night when I decided to save Alex and Edward by running away to the park instead of confronting Dad and stopping him from hitting Bryce. I believe that is the night his fate was sealed as the lost child, the child who willingly received the abuse because he didn't think he deserved any better.

Bryce just took it all. He never fought back when Dad hit him. It's as if Bryce decided that being the victim of abuse was simply his role in the world. Without complaint, he claimed this identity.

In the spring of 1990, a year or so after his first overdose, Bryce almost burned the house down. He was using a crack pipe in his bedroom and somehow set the polyester bedspread on fire. Crack was

Bryce's drug of choice because it was much cheaper than cocaine and rampantly available in DC during the late 1980s and early 1990s.

It's 1:00 a.m., and the rest of the family is asleep. I smell the smoke first; my bedroom is just down the hall from Bryce's. His bedspread is on fire, but Bryce is out of it and paralyzed in place on the floor of his bedroom.

I run in and grab him.

"Bryce! Your room is on fire! We have to get out of the house."

He doesn't seem to register anything. I drag him down the hallway.

I scream up the stairs for Debby and the other boys to wake up. "Mom, get up! Get up! The house is on fire. Get up! Grab the boys and get them out of the house."

Holding Bryce, I grasp the cordless phone in the kitchen and call 911 while shoving Bryce forward toward our front door and then out of the house. Debby, carrying Edward and Alex, rushes down the stairs and out the front door. I give our address to the 911 operator, hang up the phone, and run outside. The fire department quickly arrives and puts out the flames before they spread to other rooms in the house.

We are all outside on the sidewalk, with our neighbors, watching six firemen move in and out of our house. No one is attending to Bryce. Debby is crying and getting sympathy from the neighbors. I don't know which alter is Out, but whoever it is is not helpful.

After the fire is put out, the fire chief sits Debby and me down. He explains to us that Bryce is a drug addict and needs serious help.

"Ma'am, you need to get your son detoxed and checked into a facility. Do you need help doing that?"

Debby tells him that is nonsense, that it was only a teeny fire, and that everything is fine. Because I am barely sixteen at the time and look young for my age, I have to go along with whatever alter is saying this because she is the one who looks like an adult.

As far as I know, neither the fire chief nor anyone from social services followed up with our family or with Bryce. The house smelled like burned plastic for months. The walls in Bryce's room are blackened and left that way.

A few months later we kicked Bryce out, shortly after he turned fourteen. He stole Debby's car keys in the middle of the night and took off for a joyride. He didn't come home until much later the next day, causing Debby to miss work. The dashboard was covered with cocaine dust, and the front fender was damaged.

I forced Debby's hand that day and made her call the police. One of Debby's personalities, I'm not sure which, finally made the call I'd rehearsed in my head a thousand times. When the police cruisers arrived, our neighbors materialized on their manicured lawns like a Greek chorus, maintaining a careful distance while drinking in every detail of our latest family fracture. Their presence felt like spotlights on a stage we never asked to occupy, their whispers the soundtrack to our ongoing tragedy. This was just the newest act in our house's long-running drama of dysfunction—another scene where private pain became public theater.

The police handcuffed Bryce and bent his tall, weedy frame into the back of the squad car. He almost looked grateful, as if welcoming a respite from chasing his addiction. I watched from our doorway, the same spot where I'd stood through countless other family catastrophes, as my brother disappeared into the back of a police car.

The cocaine dust remained on the dash of the car for months because no one thought to clean it off.

24 came Out after the police left and began crying, wondering what she ever did to cause Bryce's addiction. This pity party, 24's response to everything that ever happened, continued for several hours. There was never any concern about how long Bryce would spend in jail, or informing Dad about what happened, or about how her other children were feeling about their brother being carted off.

After Bryce got out of jail, Debby's solution to Bryce's drug addiction was to send him to live with our abusive father. Dad lost his job shortly after Bryce went to live with him, and he and Bryce, both active addicts, became homeless.

CHAPTER TEN
ALEX

1989 is a summer of death for our family.

I do not blame either Alex or Bryce for not wanting to be alive. Every day in our home is brutal. School is a too-short respite, and neither Bryce nor Alex has any interest in doing schoolwork, so they mainly just go to see their friends. But now we're on summer break, so there is no distraction from home life.

Alex is six when he tells me he wants a bodyguard to protect him from Dad and Debby. He is the only one of us with blond hair and blue eyes—the rest of us have brown hair and hazel or brown eyes. He is very thin and small for his age and already too well-studied and educated for his own good. He pays attention to everything that happens, always assessing his safety. He knows he is not safe in our family. He seems to think a bodyguard will keep him safe.

The terms of our parents' separation dictate that my brothers and I have to visit with Dad and stay with him two weekends a month. The first weekend does not go well.

Edward, at almost three-years-old, is sitting on Dad's living room sofa and crying, because he always cries around our father. After an hour of constant wailing, Dad has had enough. He takes a pillow off the sofa and attempts to suffocate Edward. I jump on Dad's back, screaming and pulling at him, to get him to stop. He finally lets up, but Edward is inconsolable. I take him into my bedroom, an 8'x10' room with nothing but a single bare mattress on the floor. I curl up with him on the bed, soothing him until he falls asleep.

Later I call Debby, tell her what happened, and ask her to pick us up. She tells me she's busy and we'll have to wait for our father to bring us home the next day.

A month or so later, Bryce and Alex were at Dad's place for the weekend. Alex witnessed Dad, in another one of his alcohol-led rages, pick up twelve-year-old Bryce and throw him against the front door of his rental house.

The impact mapped across Bryce's skin in a terrible geography of blues and purples—door-shaped bruises and fingermark continents that told the story of our father's rage. For weeks, my brother wore these marks like a second skin, each bruise fading through a spectrum of colors that tracked time like a twisted calendar.

The most chilling part wasn't the violence itself but our collective response to it: nothing. We watched these marks bloom and fade on my brother's body with the same resigned acceptance we might give to a change in weather—it will pass. None of us thought to take Bryce to a doctor or clinic for medical attention. That's just not something we did in our family. In our world, wounds were family secrets, healing was a private ceremony, and pain was something to carry silently.

This was the unspoken doctrine of our household: We handle things internally, we don't seek help, we don't acknowledge the bleeding elephant in the room. It was as if seeking medical attention would somehow make the violence more real, transform just another family evening into something that existed in the outside world where people asked questions and wrote reports.

All hell broke loose with my brothers in the weeks following this event.

First, Bryce gets ahold of a bunch of drugs and takes them at school, telling his friends what he has done and that he wants to die. They drag him to the nurse's office, and the school recommends institutionalizing him in a psychiatric facility for two weeks. This is within weeks of his first overdose. He's twelve. Debby follows the school's recommendations and admits Bryce to a psychiatric institution about fifteen minutes away from our house. He seems relieved to be safe in the hospital, away from Debby and Dad.

Alex, at six, had already witnessed both Bryce and Debby attempt to end their own lives, less than a year apart, on top of Dad trying to kill Bryce. One early summer day, he announced to Debby and me that he was going to kill himself. He had seen the writing on the wall in our family, and he wanted out. Debby thought he was just mimicking what he had seen and that he didn't really want to end his own life.

This was also the summer that Debby's car died, the furnace in our house failed, and the roof leaked. Nothing in our home was immune from death and destruction.

Alex did not want to be hospitalized, but Debby said she didn't want to risk his attempting suicide and admitted him to the same psychiatric institution where Bryce was. Alex felt like Debby was hospitalizing him because she had no interest in parenting him. He was not wrong.

Dad didn't want Bryce or Alex hospitalized. He said that it would make him look bad as a parent now that he and Debby are separated.

At the hospital, Alex violently pushes chairs against the admitting nurse's desk. Two orderlies put him in a straitjacket and march him into a padded room until he calms down.

Eventually, Alex makes some friends at the hospital, starts sleeping through the night, and stops talking about his death plan. The psychiatric hospital discharges him a few weeks later. His role in our family as martyr has been solidified. He becomes the endurer of all suffering. Whatever happens in our family, or in his reality, becomes more evidence that life is only misery.

Alex seemingly ages overnight, becoming the type of older person who asks how you are but then, ninety seconds into the conversation, starts telling you about all of their ailments. Alex loves his ailments. Life becomes a litmus test of suffering, and he becomes a master casualty. This is his form of self-preservation.

Even at his tender age, Alex becomes our family's tuning fork for pain, vibrating in perfect resonance with every frequency of suffering— both personal and global. Our conversations transform into catalogs of catastrophe, each interaction a descent into his carefully curated museum of misery. It's as if he's appointed himself curator of chaos, collecting exhibits of everything broken in our world.

He starts close to home, archiving our family's daily disasters with scholarly precision: Dad's latest explosion of violence against Bryce or Debby (or both, on the really bad days); each incident he dissects and examines like evidence at a crime scene. But this domestic gallery of horrors isn't enough to contain his growing appetite for anguish. His scope expands exponentially, like a black hole consuming light.

In his teenage years, heavy metal becomes his Greek chorus, its lyrics of rage and destruction providing the perfect soundtrack to his worldview. He recites them like scripture, finding validation in every screamed verse about a world gone mad. From there, his collection grows: political elections become prophecies of doom and international conflicts transform into personal wounds he carries as if they were happening in our backyard. He counts homeless people like others count sheep, tallies nuclear warheads like baseball cards, each new statistic of suffering becomes another piece in his mosaic of despair.

Alex perfects the art of pain seeking through his childhood and into his teenage years, as if gathering evidence to prove what his family has taught him: The world is fundamentally broken, and his role is to bear witness to every crack and fissure. It's a peculiar inheritance—this compulsion to catalog catastrophe—passed down through generations of unprocessed trauma, filtered through the fractured lens of our mother's personalities and our father's alcoholic fog.

I came to rely on Alex whenever I needed to know what could be wrong with our world.

Alex also began reading books, which became a welcome distraction from our family. This eventually turned into a love affair with ten-dollar words, which Alex used in every casual conversation, often slightly incorrectly.

As adults, after we had not spoken to each other for several years, I remember Alex hearing my voice on the phone and immediately telling me that I sounded "comported."

The word comport is a verb meaning "behave." He used the word as a variable noun, not as a verb. Telling me that I sounded behaved didn't make any sense. I think he meant to use the word composed, or perhaps, coherent. It was definitely a "c" word that he was going for.

So, almost right, but not quite.

This is how all conversations went with Alex. He kept talking, while I was still trying to figure out how he had actually intended to use the sophisticated word he referenced in his previous sentence. Pseudo-intellectualism was Alex's codependent lover.

Alex dropped out of college at age eighteen during his first semester because he didn't like being tested and graded, just like Dad, and was terrified of failing. He picked up community college again when he was thirty-eight. That time he stuck it out for two semesters. He dropped out of that college during COVID-19 because his instructors wanted him to install software (Alex called it "spyware") on his computer to ensure he wasn't cheating during exams. Alex felt completely threatened by this, so rather than negotiate, he dropped out. Just like with our father, there was always a reason Alex couldn't quite ever complete things. He admitted he was a good planner but terrible at follow-through.

When he was six, Alex decided he wasn't made to live in this world. This remained the major theme for him: suffering through a life he never wanted. This was Alex's recipe for self-preservation.

CHAPTER ELEVEN

EDWARD

Edward was born twelve years after me. Of all my brothers, he is my favorite, probably because I was more than just his big sister. I was a surrogate parent from the start to this bright-eyed baby who seemed somehow untouched by our family's shadows.

I saw possibility in Edward from birth. He was expressive and full of life, with an inner light that set him apart from our darker family narrative. By the time Edward was born, Bryce was already following our father's footsteps into addiction, and Alex carried depression like a heavy cloak. Edward had an almost defiant vitality.

With Edward, I had a glimpse of what childhood should look like—full of wonder rather than hypervigilance and giggles instead of grief. In a household where survival was our primary art form, Edward dared to do more than just survive; he wanted to live. His enthusiasm wasn't just refreshing—it was revolutionary, a tiny rebellion against our family's tendency toward trauma and tragedy.

Although I didn't know it then, being both sister and surrogate mother to Edward gave me something I desperately needed: hope. I couldn't rewrite the stories of Bryce's addiction or Alex's depression. But with Edward, I could at least attempt to experience a different kind of childhood *through* him, one where the desire to live wasn't treated as suspicious behavior.

Edward was born in a tumultuous time in our family, arriving as an innocent into a storm of dysfunction. His wasn't a planned birth, and his timing seemed cruel—less than a year before Tracy's death, as if the universe wanted to ensure one more generation would carry our family's trauma.

By the time he entered our world, Dad had already become violent, his alcoholic rages a constant threat. Debby was already flirting with depression. The foundation of our family home was already cracked by trauma and fractured by Debby's multiplicity.

Edward never knew anything other than danger in our household, never experienced the illusion of safety that I had in my earliest years before everything shattered. But somehow, remarkably, he blossomed in ways I never did. While I learned to make myself small and invisible as a survival strategy, Edward moved through our dangerous world with an authenticity I couldn't risk during my years of managing Debby's alters. I am grateful that Edward didn't have to suppress himself the way I did, even as I wonder if my protective presence as his sister-mother helped create that freedom.

As a preteen, Edward chose a path different from Bryce and Alex. Instead of numbing out through drugs or drowning in suffering, he turned his attention to music. He pioneered his way into electronica, a new genre in the 1990s. Most commonly known as dance music, the genre is typically created with synthesizers and drum machines, often incorporating samples of prerecorded music or sound. It was his own form of multiple personalities, I realized later, this music that layered different sounds and identities into something whole and beautiful, so different from how Debby's alters fractured our reality.

Edward's music became his escape, his way of processing our family chaos. But it wasn't enough to save him. He also attempted suicide when he was twelve. In Debby's recollection, he tried something in junior high school: "He took ibuprofen or Tylenol. He just sort of slept it off." On the scale of suicide attempts in our family, this was not deemed worthy of concern.

Later, we figured out this flirtation with suicide was related to his struggling with his sexuality. Edward wasn't out yet, carrying this truth inside himself like a time bomb. It clearly had been weighing heavily on him. A therapist sensed the pressure building, telling us that Edward was "hiding something major." She couldn't name the specific gravity pulling at him, but she recognized its force, saw how it was eroding him from the inside out. His silence spoke volumes, though none of us yet knew how to translate its language.

When Edward was thirteen, we noticed that a monthly phone bill had an extra $200 in charges from a 900 gay sex chat number that charged by the minute to call. Because Edward hadn't had a lot of supervision (I had moved out four years before this), we didn't know if he was the responsible party. But Alex really wasn't a phone person, so I used my skills of deduction—skills honed from years of tracking Debby's different personalities—and determined that Edward was the more likely culprit.

Debby and I confront Edward about the phone calls. We are sitting on one of the two sofas in the living room that has been covered in a blue sheet by an unnamed alter I have never personally met. She appears when I'm not at home, and her sole purpose seems to be covering over our reality. I silently call her Blue. She is slowly but surely overtaking our house in shades of blue, as if trying to blanket our family's chaos in calm.

Edward is standing in front of us, in washed-out tan pants with a hole in the knee and a T-shirt promoting a band I've never heard of. He has grown out of his preadolescent pudgy stage and is now a lanky, nearly six-foot-tall, almost-adult. His feet are huge. Everything about him is so different from the little boy version of him I always picture in my mind.

He is the most nervous I have ever seen him. He doesn't want to admit he made the phone calls.

Debby and I had already discussed the possibility of Edward being gay. On some level we had known for years. This seemed like the perfect opportunity to finally discuss it with him. I asked Edward directly if he was gay. He looked down at his feet and shrugged. I took that for as close to an admission as we might get from him.

Debby's alters keep switching in during this conversation, each one needing to share their thoughts about Edward being gay, creating a chorus of acceptance that might have seemed bizarre to outsiders but was perfectly normal in our household.

24, always the one to point out the negative side of things, says, "You know, it's really hard to be gay in this world. It's good that we are supporting you."

Five, still a child herself, and her motivation always being to play, says, "Are you still going to play with us even though you like boys now?"

At one point I blurt out, "We're so happy for you, honey. It's okay. We support you." For a moment there, it seemed like Edward thought we wouldn't love him or back him, as if a family accommodating all of Debby's personalities couldn't make room for one more truth.

In the following years, Edward grew into himself, both as a gay man and as an artist.

In 2004, when he is eighteen and I am thirty, I give him a surprise high school graduation present. We fly to London for a week to explore the city's electronic music scene. It's such a new concept to me that I don't understand a performance by an electronic musician is simply a guy standing on a stage in front of a laptop, connected to speakers. (I inadvertently sat on the stage at the first show because I didn't realize the show had started.)

I get to be a part of Edward's world for a few days. He and I bond even more deeply during this trip. He finds my naivete amusing, and patiently explains electronica to me for the fifteenth time after that concert, even though he knows it will go in one ear and out the other, because the concept is so foreign to me. To Edward, I am his mother, and he treats me as such during this trip. I am an older, slower person who is unable to understand modern technology.

I find Edward's patience with me endearing. He knows I'm trying to be hip and cool, but our twelve-year age difference and the rapid speed of technology create a huge gap between our respective orientations in the technological world. Yet this gap feels different from the one created by Debby's alters—it's a gap of progress rather than trauma.

In adulthood Edward became a professional DJ and electronica musician, performing in venues throughout the Washington, DC, metropolitan area. When Edward was twenty-eight, he married Ben, once it was finally legal for same-sex couples to marry in DC. They had a Quaker wedding at our Meetinghouse, followed by a giant party at a music venue in the city. Edward and Ben both wore fabulous bright red suits and flaunted their identities as gay married men. I was so proud of Edward for knowing who he was and what he wanted. It was a clarity I helped protect during the years when I was more mother than sister, ensuring he had space to become himself.

CHAPTER TWELVE

SACRIFICE

Much of the parenting in our family falls to me after my parents separate. Dad is largely unavailable, consumed by his own depression and alcoholism. He occasionally makes child support payments for the first year, but then those payments disappear, and we are solely reliant on Debby's salary to survive.

I begin my days at 4:30 a.m., bagging newspapers I deliver to seventy homes in our neighborhood before 6:00. I come home, shower, eat breakfast, and make school lunches for all four of us. I get the boys up by 6:45 so we can be out the door by 7:30. After school I help them with their homework, forging signatures on permission slips when I can't get Debby to function. I make dinner. I read books to Edward. I teach Alex how to do multiplication. I begin my own homework after I put them to bed at 8:00 or 9:00 p.m. Most nights, I don't fall asleep until midnight. On weekends I clean the house, mow the grass, and wash and fold loads of laundry. I try to spend time with Alex and Edward, playing games with them, or taking them to the park.

Within two years of 24's suicide attempt, Debby admitted herself to a psychiatric institution for three weeks. This occurred in the fall of 1989, shortly after Bryce and Alex were hospitalized in the children's ward of the same institution. That fall, Debby spent most evenings and weekends in bed or as an inpatient at psychiatric institutions.

Debby somehow managed to hold down a job as an editor during this time. I can only guess it's because she was exceptional at manipulating other people and must have figured out how to manipulate her boss to keep him from firing her for all the time she kept taking off from work. He must have felt sorry for her instead of thinking she was crazy. Or there were alters that came out to function during the day at her job and then conveniently disappeared at home when it was time for her to take care of her family. It doesn't matter how she pulled it off, really. We needed her salary and health insurance in order to survive as a family.

Debby's revolving door relationship with psychiatric wards spanned my adolescence into early adulthood, a decade punctuated by admission bracelets and discharge papers. From my fifteenth birthday through my college graduation, I marked time by hospital visits rather than holidays, learning to navigate life while my mother drifted in and out of institutions like a ghost haunting sterile hallways.

Years later, when I was old enough to ask the hard questions, Debby offered me a metaphor as weightless as smoke: She was "underwater," she said, her voice carrying the practiced distance of someone describing someone else's life. This convenient drowning narrative wrapped a decade of absence in the gauzy language of dissociation. It's a masterful sleight of hand—transforming years of chaos and abandoned motherhood into a poetic state of suspension, as if she were Ophelia floating in a stream rather than a mother who left her children to navigate the turbulent waters of trauma alone.

The irony doesn't escape me: While she was "underwater," I was learning to breathe for all of us—myself, my three brothers, and her boatload of personalities. Her metaphorical submersion became our literal sink-or-swim reality.

I coped by numbing out and going through the motions of living, completely incapable of accessing my own emotions or needs. For the period of Debby's depression, from 1987 to 1996, I was in my own dissociated state—reserved and inaccessible. A shell of a person, I existed only to keep my family alive. This was not resilience or fortitude. It was a conscious choice not to become suicidal like Debby and my brothers or a depressive alcoholic like Dad.

I am navigating a landscape of the living dead—a world where my family shuffles through existence like extras in a tragedy they've accepted as normal. My father drowns himself in alcohol, my mother exists only in fragments, my brothers each perfect their own forms of slow surrender: addiction, depression, obsession with suffering.

I am living in my family's horrifying world, where no one wants to be alive. Except me. I want to live. It doesn't occur to me not to live. Just like Bryce has mastered numbing out with drugs and Alex has mastered becoming a casualty of suffering, I master being in charge and dragging everyone in my family, kicking and screaming, into remaining alive with me. My desire to live grows simply as a default mechanism for keeping my family in the land of the living.

At fifteen, I tried to convince my driver's education teacher to let me get my driver's license before other students in my class. Debby was institutionalized for close to a month, and I couldn't figure out how to do the grocery shopping without a car because we lived in the suburbs, miles from a grocery store.

In my most adult, calm voice, I explained to my teacher, "I need to get my driver's license immediately. My mother is sick, and I can't get to the grocery store." It was important to me that I come across as having it together, and that I was being responsible, so this woman could understand that my request was sincere.

The teacher doesn't seem to believe me about my mother being sick, so I break down in tears. "But I have no one to help me! My mother is in the hospital, and we've run out of food!" I cry. The tears are for her, not me. I never cry, I am cold and calculating—my best self-preservation technique.

Even the tears don't work with this woman. I have to wait to take the test. The teacher seems remarkably unconcerned that my mother is in the hospital, that my siblings and I have no other adult to care for us, and that we are out of food. She's hell-bent on enforcing her rules. Recruiting some of my classmates to support me in getting my license first and relinquishing their turns doesn't work either, although my friends eagerly want to help.

That was one of the few times I directly asked an adult for help with my family, and I was turned down. This reinforced that I was on my own in dealing with our family chaos.

I got my driver's license five weeks later, on the same day I ended up driving Debby to a different psychiatric institution to have her admitted. This was less than a month after her previous institutionalization.

The scene that still haunts me in my dreams:

We are in a family therapy session at one of the psychiatric institutions. In the room are a middle-aged male therapist devoid of personality and Debby, seated next to each other in matching Baker-Miller Pink industrial chairs with wooden legs, the type I only ever see in hospitals.

The psychology of color is based on the mental and emotional effects colors have on people in all facets of life, including cognition and behavior. Baker-Miller Pink is a paint color that reportedly reduces hostile, violent, or aggressive behavior. It was developed in 1979 in Seattle, Washington, for a naval correctional institute to study the impact of pink prison cells on inmates. It's named for the institute's directors at the time, Baker and Miller.

We're in a small room, with just enough space for the two chairs and a three-seater beige couch, with itchy fabric and hard seats. The walls of the room are also beige. There is a painting on the wall with the same shade of pink in it. The therapist wears a beige shirt, which matches the beige couch and his lack of personality.

I wonder to myself if Blue, the alter who is deeply devoted to re-covering our furniture at home in shades of blue, refuses to come out when she is in this beige room.

My three brothers and I are all squeezed together on the couch, with me in the middle, holding Edward. We are listening to the therapist explain that we "need to be more understanding and considerate of Debby's condition." "You should be nicer to her at home," the therapist says, "and not always put so much stress on her." Debby is nodding her head and smiling at the therapist.

The session continues, but all I remember is deciding in that moment that I would be who Debby needed me to be, that I would stop existing for my own sake.

At a time when most of my peers were vying for their independence and working out who they were as individuated beings, I shut down that impulse. While other eleventh graders were choosing prom dresses and college majors, my rite of passage became saving our family by ignoring my own needs and stage of growth. In my already numbed state, I didn't analyze this choice—I just decided to annihilate myself at barely sixteen years old. Another attempt at self-preservation in a household where Debby had already split into pieces to preserve herself.

I couldn't and didn't comprehend the long-term ramifications of the silent choice I made to eradicate myself that day in the therapist's office or that my partial death would still haunt me decades later, emerging in unexpected ways, or that I might never fully become my own independent self, and that after mothering my brothers I would eventually have to learn to mother myself back to wholeness.

After we meet with the therapist, I gather up my brothers and drive us all home. I can tell the therapy session was hard for them too. They bicker in the car. Edward starts wailing. We are all tired and hungry. I want to do something nice for them.

I make us dinner—macaroni and cheese with pieces of ham in it—because the boys all love it. The meal is quick to make, which helps because I now have a migraine that is pounding its way into thwarting my ability to multitask. The migraines are the physical manifestation of carrying not just my brothers' needs but also the weight of navigating Debby, and they are becoming more frequent, at least twice a week now. They are my body's way of compensating for the emotional stress.

To relieve the pain and pressure in my neck and back, which get so tense during my migraines, I lie on my stomach on the thready oriental rug in the living room, another hand-me-down in a house full of borrowed normalcy. The boys know the drill when I do this and what their role is in this "game" we play when I am wracked with pain. Like so many things in our household, we've turned trauma into routine, crisis into play. This is the only time I ever let my guard down—when the physical pain becomes too much to maintain the careful control required to manage our fractured family dynamic. I issue the challenge: "Okay, who wants to walk on my back tonight?" Edward and Alex both love this fun game, like seeing which one can crack my back first. They're still little boys, weighing under sixty pounds—not enough to damage my back but enough to relieve some pressure. In these moments, their innocence becomes my medicine.

"I wanna go first!" Edward replies. He jumps on my back with both feet, his childish enthusiasm a stark contrast to the careful way I must navigate Debby's

alters. He knows not to step on my spine—even at four, he's learned to care for his sister-mother. Then he walks up and down my back for a few minutes before getting bored and wandering off.

The pain is still there, so I call out to Alex. "Hey Ax! Get on my back!" He's a little more strategic and digs his heels into my scapulae. There's the relief I've been waiting for. For the first time in hours, I stop holding my breath—a brief respite from being the family's anchor. "Don't move; that's the perfect spot." Alex, ever the know-it-all, even at this tender age, says, "I know, Em, that's why I'm doing it."

After a five-minute break from excruciating pain, I hug Alex hard and thank him. Then I find Edward and do the same. I talk Bryce into washing the dishes so I can spend that time helping Alex with his math homework. I give Edward a bath and get him into bed by 8:30. Then I get Alex settled in his bed and tell him he can read until 9:00. Reading is his favorite activity, so he is content. The evening routine continues, regardless of my pain.

I still have my homework to do, but I can't keep my eyes open. Partially because I'm so tired, but the migraines also make me extremely sensitive to light. I get ice out of the freezer and make myself an ice pack for the back of my head, where my migraine lives. The trays are only half full, but enough ice fills a small baggie. I refill them completely before putting myself to bed—one last act of preparation for whatever tomorrow might bring, whichever version of Debby might greet us.

When I share some of these childhood stories, one of the first questions people ask is whether Child Protective Services was involved. In the 1980s, of course, things were much different for children. We were Generation X—the proud and free latchkey kids––the generation that took care of ourselves while both parents worked. We were the generation that knew how to be alone at home after school, often shouldering parental responsibilities because our parents spent a lot of time outside the home earning a living. My stories of making family dinners or helping my brothers with their homework weren't unusual.

In my adolescence, I assumed that what I was doing wasn't a big deal. There wasn't judgment or upset that I was taking on these huge responsibilities. I didn't complain about them, and perhaps that's part of why I was able to fly under the radar, never soliciting outside support. Most of what I was doing wasn't unusual or remarkable.

Taking four-year-old Edward with me to high school for the day because my mother was in a psychiatric institution, my father was unavailable, and Edward's daycare was unexpectedly closed—*that* was unusual. I don't know why none of my teachers asked why I had my little brother with me in all of my classes. Why wasn't a guidance counselor notified when Bryce showed up at school with bruises on his face and track marks in his arms from heroin usage?

Was I just that good at covering for my family? Was I able to clean up the mess just enough to make things look normal? Or was it too complicated to interfere with the massive dysfunction that was our family? Because Child Protective Services was never called.

Some people occasionally stepped in to tend to us. A few women from our Quaker meeting sometimes came over when Debby was hospitalized, and they helped me with laundry, cooking, and cleaning up around the house. I spent time with a family from our old neighborhood when I needed a dose of mothering. Susan, a good friend of Debby's from work, stayed at the house with Alex and Edward after I graduated from high school. Susan had a particular fondness for Alex, and they became close through their shared love of reading. There was a man from our Quaker meeting who became a mentor to Edward when he got older, helping him grow his interest in music.

However, no one ever intervened to advocate for us kids and get us out of that situation. Nor did our father. No one said to me, "Emma, this is not okay. You need help, and I am going to help you. You are not alone here. This is not your job. You deserve to be a kid." I learned too young that asking for help was futile, so I shouldered every burden alone—becoming my own cavalry, my own support system, my own solution to problems no child should have to solve.

From 1987 to 1996, our family existed in a perpetual state of emergency, like survivors of an invisible war that no one else could see or understand. Those nine years stretched before us like a minefield, where every day brought the possibility of a new personality emerging from the fractured landscape of our mother's psyche and every night held the threat of another suicide attempt.

Debby was undergoing what her therapists called "integration"—a process that, in retrospect, felt more like psychological archaeology gone wrong. The therapeutic fashion of the time insisted on excavating every buried trauma, forcing her to relive each horror as if fresh wounds might somehow heal old scars. This brutal approach to healing turned our mother into both archaeologist and artifact, each dig bringing up new alters like shards of a shattered mirror, each piece reflecting a different fragment of her broken past.

We had no roadmap for this territory. Multiple personality disorder—as it was called then—remained more mystery than diagnosis, leaving us to navigate with no compass. While Debby disappeared into the labyrinth of her therapy sessions, allegedly working toward wholeness, we children were left motherless for all intents and purposes, watching her fragment into distinct personalities. Each new alter that emerged was another piece of evidence that our mother was simultaneously everywhere and nowhere, present in body but scattered across the geography of her own mind.

The irony of integration therapy was that it seemed to multiply rather than unify. Every uncovered trauma spawned new alters, like a hydra growing two heads for each one cut off. My brothers and I became unwitting experts in this psychological multiplication, learning to read the subtle signs of personality shifts the way other children learned to read books.

PART 4
RESCUE
(1990–1992)

CHAPTER THIRTEEN

JOHN

By 1990, Debby was still in therapy but actively dating. She brought a couple of men home for us to meet. They were inconsequential and uninteresting. I could tell they wouldn't stick. Even Debby was bored in their presence. Then she started dating John. I discovered this when I walked into Debby's bedroom one Saturday morning to ask her when she was going to get up and start helping with the boys.

Everything about John irritates me. At six feet, four inches, he is too tall. His nose is too big, his tone too serious, his skin too pale, his self-aggrandizement is disturbing, and Debby's obsession with him is revolting.

I cannot for the life of me figure out what Debby sees in this guy. Somehow he has taken on the role of hero with all of the alters. They love him, treat him as their personal confidante, and trust him completely. Meanwhile, John moves into our house while Debby financially supports him.

John is very white collar and very erudite. Everyone takes him seriously, except me. John is supposedly a "consultant" for companies in the DC area, but I never see him actually work. Nevertheless, his desk and bookshelves have taken over the back room of our house, and he is occupying Debby's bed. Debby never tells us that he has moved in. I just came home one day from school, and all of John's stuff was in our house.

The back room—named with the same tired resignation that marks much of our lives—stands as a testament to misguided ambition. It clings to the main house like an architectural afterthought, the previous owners' fumbled attempt at grandeur in the form of a sunroom. Their dreams of sun-drenched sophistication resulted in something more akin to a glorified shed, where cheap wood paneling desperately tries to masquerade as warmth.

Ten windows march along the walls in rigid formation, each four feet by thirty inches of bargain-basement glass that manages to both invite and distort the outside world. They create a fishbowl effect, as if we're living in a display case. During summer, the room transforms into a greenhouse of stifling secrets. In winter, it shivers with poorly insulated regret.

The exterior door—its frame slightly askew due to moisture and humidity—opens to what could generously be called a staircase. In reality, it's a decaying wooden cascade, each step softening with rot, descending precariously into our unkempt backyard. We've developed an unspoken family protocol about these stairs: Pretend they don't exist, just as we pretend not to notice so many other deteriorating aspects of our lives. The steps have become another metaphor we live with—something that once promised access to a better space, now too dangerous to trust.

John fills the back room with an impressive set of walnut bookshelves and a giant wooden desk, with the specially crafted addition of cubbies to hold pens, paper clips, and other tools of his consulting trade. The dining table, which had occupied that room since we moved in, big enough for our entire family to actually sit around, disappeared the same day John moved in. Now the six of us sit around the cramped kitchen table, only big enough for four people.

John's one redeeming quality is that he has made it his personal mission to get Debby properly diagnosed. This is also my personal mission, but because I am only sixteen, no one is taking me seriously. Debby's doctors won't return my calls. Neither will her health insurance company or her therapist.

John doesn't help with managing our household or dealing with practical day-to-day realities. Taking over Debby's management becomes his self-appointed full-time job. Despite my feelings about John, I am delighted to have a brief hiatus from managing Debby while he lives with us.

By the time John moves in, Debby has been seeing a therapist for three years. He is meek and slight, well-meaning, with an office situated in a Presbyterian church, complete with a steeple and stained-glass windows. The church is equidistant between our house and the house Debby grew up in with Tracy, where my grandfather Frank still lives.

The therapist is punching above his weight class with Debby. He's never had a client with alternative personalities. But they feel safe with him, so Debby still sees him once a week.

John accompanies Debby to the therapist to discuss her situation and assess next steps, because the therapist has already indicated she needs more advanced help than he is able to provide. The psychiatric institution down the road from our house, where Debby spent three weeks last fall, recommends a new therapist who has experience working with multiples. The new therapist is across the river in Washington, DC, at the Psychiatric Institute of Washington. John and Debby's current therapist agree she should go for evaluation and a formal diagnosis of multiple personality disorder. The alters comply. They always submit to what John tells them to do.

Finally, there was movement. John's efforts to rescue Debby resulted in getting qualified support for her disorder. I wondered if this meant that Debby would stop being suicidal, and catatonic, and unavailable all of the time. But it didn't. Things got worse before they got better.

CHAPTER FOURTEEN

ANNA

Anna is blowing cigarette smoke in my face.

"Anna, stop blowing smoke in my face. It causes cancer, you know," I say to her. I want to join her in the living room to read a book, but I can't when the room is full of smoke. It makes me gag. She doesn't respond, just keeps blowing. I guess Anna doesn't believe me.

Anna started smoking as a teenager in the 1960s and is trapped in that reality. She came into existence during an age when over 40 percent of adults smoked. For her, smoking is a way of being. It keeps her calm and gives her purpose.

The alter Anna is seventeen years old. I assume, like all of the other alters, that her age reflects the year in which she was formed—in this case, when Debby was seventeen.

It's now 1990, and Anna is Out a lot. I don't remember seeing her when I was younger.

Anna likes to sit in Debby's chair in the living room when she smokes. Blue recently re-covered the chair, on a weekend day when I was out of the house. The room is now consumed by various shades of sky and navy blue.

Anna's purse is on the floor next to the chair so she can easily access her cigarettes. The chair was a hand-me-down from a friend of Tracy's. It has a big seat, wide armrests, and a slightly reclined back, so it is very comfortable to sit in. Anna's legs are curled up under her, in a teenage, I-don't-care-what-I-look-like stance. She can sit in that chair and stare out our large picture window for hours. I have no idea what she looks at.

The window framed a view of half-dead boxwoods, smushed together in a row to hide our front porch from the neighbors. The porch was really just a three-foot by eight-foot strip of concrete to the right of the front door. Beyond the boxwoods were our neighbors across the street. Their yellow house was perched atop a steep slope, distancing it from the road.

Ours was a lower middle-class suburban neighborhood in the DC area, noted for its racial and ethnic diversity. When we moved in a few years before, the house was occupied by a Mexican family, but recently a Pakistani family moved in. On this particular day, there was no activity in their yard, which was usually filled with children. Nothing was happening at the house to its left either, which was occupied by a Black family whose yard also typically buzzed with the sounds of children playing. It was late, after dinnertime for most of the families on our road. Everyone was already inside for the evening. So Anna, per usual, was staring at nothing.

My role with most of the alters was clear: I was the parent because they either were too young to know how or they were older than me and in so much pain that they were unable to function. But it was different with Anna. She was only two years older than me, so we functioned more as peers. I didn't need to parent her, and she didn't parent me. We just coexisted, not really friends or family or anything. She was more formed than some of the other personalities. But I couldn't figure out exactly how to be in relationship with her. I couldn't even remember when or how I learned her name.

Anna is completely self-absorbed, a way of existing that feels foreign to me. She is the very worst of an adolescent girl. Completely stubborn, she will not listen to reason. She always leads with her own agenda, which doesn't include helping me get anything accomplished. I have found it easier to be complacent and just do what needs to get done so things don't escalate. There is no deep turmoil within me about this; it's just the way things are.

What Anna mainly cares about is getting her own needs met. Mealtime falls by the wayside when Anna is around because she doesn't eat. So cooking dinner is now added to my roster of daily tasks. I can make spaghetti, a homemade version of Hamburger Helper we call Nancy's Favorite Casserole (I have no idea who Nancy is), tacos, and macaroni and cheese. These are all foods that my brothers will eat, so there isn't fighting at the dinner table about having to eat three bites before I let them leave the table.

Thanks to Anna's frequent presence, I become an exceptional multitasker during this time—raising my brothers, running a household, getting straight A's in high school, and getting up at 4:30 every morning for my newspaper route. I use the money from distributing *The Washington Post* to pay for clothes and any other hygienic products I need, aside from Prell shampoo and Irish Spring soap. These are the two things Debby purchases in bulk for the bathroom I share with my brothers.

To this day, I cannot stand the smell of Irish Spring.

No one teaches me that I need to wear deodorant once I become a teenager or to wash my feet when they get dirty. Adolescence lands me with stinky armpits, and I don't know what to do. I wash them in the shower, but by the afternoon they are foul again. I observe my peers keeping deodorant in their lockers to apply between classes. I buy the same deodorant that another girl in my class uses and apply it religiously.

One friend is obsessed with how her feet look, so I figure out from her that washing feet is a thing that people do. She is always painting her toenails during free periods, so I try that too. I buy a nail polish kit at the drugstore that has five different pastel colors—blue, green, pink, yellow, and orange. I apply a different color to each toe on both feet. My feet look fabulous. I smile every time I look down at them.

Another friend teaches me how to deal with my menstrual cycle, showing me a box of products her mother got in anticipation of her getting her period soon. She talks me through each of the products, just like her mother showed her. I go to the store and buy what I need. Another friend who already has her period stands outside the stall in the school bathroom, coaching me when I insert a tampon for the first time.

I buy a razor to shave my legs because apparently this is also a thing girls do. A girlfriend shows me how to use it. I buy some soap that smells nice to wash my feet with. I purchase conditioner for my hair. Other girls in my class talk about the importance of conditioning to prevent "split ends," whatever the hell those are. That is something I have never considered, and don't want to care about, but when these girls huddle together to discuss their hair, conditioning seems like a life-or-death situation, so I pay attention.

I read the instructions on the back of the bottle of the Salon Selectives conditioner to figure out how to apply it to my hair. It smells like candy. I feel fancy when my hair is conditioned.

I guess I could have asked Anna about all of this hygienic stuff, but to be honest, it never occurred to me. I never experience Anna as particularly helpful with my needs.

On grocery day, if Anna is Out, I have to remind her to go buy food, and I have to go with her to load up the cart. If not, she will come home with just cigarettes and coffee.

"Anna," I tell her, "We're out of food. We've got to go to the grocery store." Anna rolls her eyes, her general response whenever I suggest she do anything. "How can we already be out of food? We just went to the store."

I have never once witnessed Anna eating. She is anorexic and she's Out so often that Debby is rapidly losing weight. Most of Debby's clothes don't fit her anymore.

Anna cares deeply about the clothes she wears and has a particular love of hats. Her wardrobe mimics what Princess Diana wore during the 1980s—she likes flowered dresses, shoulder pads (Anna thinks her shoulders are "too droopy"), and wide-brimmed hats. Anna wears a size nine shoe, but all of Debby's shoes are size ten, so Anna stuffs toilet paper or newspaper into the toes of the shoes to make them fit. At one point Anna somehow even manages to wear her grandmother Nana's white lace gloves, a magnificent feat considering Debby's hands are much larger than her grandmother's were.

Anna can spend hours, and I mean hours, discussing anything superficial. A few of her favorite topics include whether her shoes match her outfit, makeup, boys, and smoking.

She wants to hear about the guys I am dating. "So, tell me about the boys at school. Who do you like?" I don't date anyone during high school, so this is always a short conversation.

"But who will you go to the dance with?" Anna asks this in a panicked voice, like the world might end if I don't have a date. The other alters don't even seem to notice I am in my junior year.

I do try to pay attention to her advice about makeup, but I don't really wear it, so her advice doesn't make a lot of sense to me. She keeps talking about something called an applicator.

"Emma, everyone knows that you need an applicator to put on foundation. Without foundation your face will only ever look rugged and unkempt. I don't understand why you aren't taking this more seriously."

Anna affects a high, lilting, pseudo-British dialect in her speech. She speaks as though she is British royalty, in no rush for a sentence to leave her mouth, because she knows she has everyone's attention—
—a stark contrast to the rushed, anxious energy that characterizes many of Debby's other alters. Most of the personalities have traceable behaviors and patterns that connect directly to our family trauma: Ten's rage echoes Tracy's abuse, Five carries the innocence Debby lost too young, Blue covers our reality in protective sheets. But Anna does not fit this pattern.

I cannot connect her body language, dialect, facial expressions, or agenda with anyone else in our family or with Debby's upbringing. While other alters clearly emerged to handle specific traumas— protecting Debby from grandfather George's voyeuristic gaze or Dad's alcoholic rages—Anna seems to have materialized from pure imagination, as if Debby's fractured psyche needed to create at least one personality completely untouched by our family's legacy of abuse. Perhaps Anna represents the escape Debby couldn't physically make— —fleeing not just to another place but to another identity entirely, one with the confidence and authority her real life never allowed.

Anna ponders questions such as "How wide should a hat brim be for different occasions?" No one fucking cares, Anna, I think to myself. No one we know, other than Anna, wears hats other than baseball caps. But I sit next to her and listen carefully because I know that eventually Anna will throw me a bone and tell me something useful about the alters.

This is how I learn that Anna is the watcher/observer among the alters. She knows everything that is happening on the Inside (of Debby's mind). Sometimes she moves things around in there—she'll regroup bunches of children, for example, or create new places for alters to live Inside.

Anna describes the Inside as a giant house with lots of rooms. Her description is more like this, though: "Oh you know, there is a house where all of us live." Like there is something fundamentally wrong with me that I don't already understand that there is a house inside of Debby.

Anna was also the one who decided which alters emerged on the Outside, when, and for how long. (The Outside is where people like you and I exist in physical form.)

If an alter on the Outside was struggling, Anna went to the "front door" of the "house" inside of Debby's mind, observed what was happening, and sent someone else Out to take their place.

On the Inside she was like an NFL coach, deciding what players are on the field, and what the plays would be. She was the rescuer, keeping Debby safe. But on the Outside, Anna manifested as lazy and unhelpful as a parent or adult.

Anna was the one who first told me about Debby's diagnosis of multiple personality disorder (known more commonly today as dissociative identity disorder).

"Debby's therapist and I have been discussing the situation. He says that she has multiple personality disorder. I told him I don't know anything about that, but I do know there are too many people on the Inside."

Anna doesn't reveal anything more. I wait a minute, then ask, "Why are there so many people inside of Mom?"

"Oh, you know how it is," Anna says, taking a long, slow drag on her Marlboro Lights cigarette, her third in the last hour.

This is how most of Anna's sentences began: "Oh, you know…"

No, I don't know, which was why I had to ask a million questions to get any level of detail out of her.

I have no idea what she is talking about. To myself, I scream, "NO, I have NO idea how it is. You never tell me anything!" But all Anna observes is me sitting quietly next to her, waiting patiently for her to share more.

"Debby had to cope with all of the abuse. That's why we are all here. To protect her. To hold the memories. That is our job."

She states this as if she is a plant manager describing the role of each of the workers on the floor. Some are here to man the machines, others, to keep things moving on the conveyor belt, and all to do their jobs. She says all this as if this is perfectly obvious and I am mentally challenged and unable to comprehend.

Anna is always without affect. Everything to her is no big deal, whether it's the dissolution of Debby's marriage, the abuse Debby endured at the hands of her mother or husband, or today's weather report. So I never know what to take seriously when Anna is Out. Everything seems the same.

"Tell me more about that," is all I dare myself to say to Anna.

She glances at me, cooly, taking yet another long drag on her cigarette. This time she stares at me as she blows the smoke from her lips straight into my eyes. I don't blink. I don't want to give her any indication that I am upset because she has now signaled to me that she is irritated and could disappear at any moment. Anna hates direct, pointed questions that require her to give up too much information.

Eventually, she relents, "Oh, you know, Debby has been deeply depressed since the mother [Tracy] died. She can't deal with all of the memories. That makes it unsafe for all of us right now. So I began reorganizing things on the Inside. I've put the children into groups, and each group has its own room. I've put many of them to sleep, so they won't keep trying to come Out."

After Tracy's death, many of the alters wanted to be on the Outside. They finally felt safe—their primary abuser was gone. But they also wanted to tell their stories and share their pain, and Debby's physical body couldn't handle the constant switching of personalities. So Anna took over and became the watcher/observer, deciding what would happen on the Outside.

From Anna's perspective, the alters had been there for Debby's whole life, but many of them, apart from a core group of about a dozen, retreated to the Inside after they were formed in response to a traumatic event. Most of them were babies, or under age four, and completely unable to function on the Outside in an adult body, so they never came Out to be observed by other people.

"Each time abuse occurred, Debby split. She got into the habit of doing this," Anna said, "and the abuse was so frequent, that countless alternative personalities were formed."

Anna and I are sitting on the front porch of our house when she tells me this. We're in metal folding chairs, with checkered yellow and white woven seats and backs—yet more hand-me-down furniture. It is sunny outside and a warmish spring day. It's late afternoon, and I know I should be inside preparing dinner. But I am having the conversation I didn't even know until this moment I had been waiting my entire life to have. To finally understand why Debby is the way she is.

The chairs are rickety and cracked, and you'll fall through them if you're not careful. I'm holding myself up, away from the chair, to avoid this while I'm trying my best to prompt Anna to tell me more, without showing her my eagerness, because as soon as she knows you want something she goes into teenage shutdown. I am tiptoeing on the eggshells of this personality.

This is a perfect analogy for how I'm feeling about my life right now—my daily practice of not falling through the cracks of Debby.

Tracy has been dead for three years, and Dad moved out over a year ago. Our household has been in total chaos for three years, and this diagnosis of Debby is the first thing that has made sense.

Of course there are alters. Of course that's why Debby never remembers anything I tell her. Of course that's why she's "checked out" most of the time. Of course that's why she's suicidal. Debby's got a train full of people moving in and out of her body at rapid speed.

"But how did this happen?" I ask Anna. "How did Debby get to be this way?" Anna tells me that Tracy sexually abused Debby from when she was little up through the end of elementary school and that Tracy was also part of a cult that ritually abused Debby. Anna tells me this with the same tone she uses when asking me to get her cigarettes out of her purse: bland and neutral.

Part of me was thrilled when Debby was first diagnosed as we finally had an explanation for what was happening. But most of me just felt shame.

I only told a few very close friends about the diagnosis because I didn't want to admit that things were so bad with Debby. I didn't want people to associate me with her mental illness or with my father's alcoholism. I needed other people, especially adults, to see me as capable and competent, as someone who kept our home functioning and my brothers safe while Debby was perpetually unavailable. Being the overly competent teenager who held everything together was my way of keeping our family intact. It was my way of surviving. I numbed myself out, ignored my own emotions, and kept our family alive with everything I had.

CHAPTER FIFTEEN
DEBBIE SUE

I open the crooked mudroom door that connects our driveway to the kitchen. There is a crowd of shoes, jackets, and recycling crammed into the three-foot by six-foot space. The walls are oddly plastered with blue and peach flowered shiny bathroom wallpaper. I immediately smell scrapple cooking.

The mudroom was built as a nonpermitted addition by the previous owners of the house. The door, like our basement door, hung with a two-inch gap separating it from the floor and is also crooked, so it had become almost impossible to close. Bugs and mice had easy access to the tin cans and plastic containers covered in food remnants that we stuffed into an overflowing plastic trash bin we used to separate recycling from the rest of the trash. No one ever remembered to take the recycling out on trash day.

There was another door from the mudroom into the kitchen. This door had a lock on it, but since the bugs and mice had already made it this far, and because the boys always forgot to close the kitchen door, we were constantly finding creatures all over the house. We were never protected, even when this door was closed.

I can smell the mix of iron and pork before I enter the kitchen. I know that Debbie Sue is Out. She is the only one of the alters who cooks scrapple.

We met Debbie Sue after Tracy died and Dad moved out. She conveniently showed up with her cooking skills when Debby was often too depressed to function. She rescued us by serving as a mother figure when we most needed it.

When I was fourteen, I claimed vegetarianism for myself because I was tired of eating half-raw chicken for dinner. Most of the alters were terrible cooks (if they even cooked), and this was how I found a way to eat food without insulting them. But Debbie Sue didn't know this. She was hardly ever on the Outside.

Debbie Sue believes that scrapple comes directly from the heavens. According to her, it is the perfect food and must be consumed daily to strengthen your constitution. I'm excited to see so much food being prepared in the kitchen, and so glad to see Debbie Sue, that I will eat anything she puts in front of me.

The kitchen is awash with activity. Every inch of the countertops is covered. A dozen eggs have made their way into the cast-iron skillet, with the blue Styrofoam egg carton thrown aside by the sink. A mound of pancakes on a plate rests next to the stove, covered with a piece of aluminum foil. The rest of that counter is dusted in flour, as is Debbie Sue's left cheek. A greasy cutting board reveals its role in slicing scrapple, now sizzling on the stove. The sink is full of peeled potato skins and eggshells.

Alex is kneeling on the counter next to the fridge, rooting around in the cupboard for Tabasco sauce. Edward is sitting on the dirty kitchen floor, playing with a toy truck.

Only a few minutes after I get home, after a twelve-hour day of high school and my after-school job at a local insurance company, dinner is ready.

Breakfast for dinner is Debbie Sue's favorite meal. The food is laid out on a wrinkled and stained blue and pink checkered tablecloth, which permanently covers the old wooden four-person kitchen table in our dining nook—an eight-foot cubby crammed between the front door and the kitchen. There isn't enough room for our bodies to fit in the chairs wrapped around the table.

We pull the table out into the hallway to eat dinner together.

We fall into a satisfied silence, a moment of harmony. We soak our scrapple in pancake syrup. The combination of the salty meat and the sweetness of maple tastes like home. Butter is slathered on each layer of pancake. The eggs get doused in Tabasco sauce, even though

Debbie Sue is the only one who likes to eat eggs that way. The fried potatoes are bathed in ketchup.

The ketchup bottle farts when we squeeze it, which makes all of us giggle. Debbie Sue roars with laughter, using her whole body to emit the sound.

The boys and I wolf the food down, while Debbie Sue looks us straight in the eyes and announces, "Y'all gonna git to yer homework right after this, ya hear? Then, everyone gits baths. No arguments."

We nod our heads and agree with her.

Debbie Sue is big and loud. She was raised in Oklahoma and has a strong Okie accent. She wears wrinkled flannel shirts and blue jeans. Somehow she is taller than Debby, her face is wider, and her hair is curlier. Despite the forty-year-old body she inhabits, she looks older, more like my grandmother Tracy would look if she were still alive and living in Oklahoma on the farm.

I close my eyes and imagine that red dirt sweeps across open plains outside our dining room window.

I am sixteen, and it is the fall of my senior year. I am applying to colleges. My aunt (Debby's sister), a college professor, sent me a guide, marking the schools she thinks I will like the best. She offers to take me on a tour of colleges in New England, which thrills and delights me. With Debbie Sue on the Outside, I know I can spend the evening working on my college essays instead of helping Alex with his homework and Edward with bath time.

Debbie Sue is one of the few alters who actually signs our permission slips for school, but we always have to remind her to sign them "Debby" instead of "Debbie Sue" so our teachers won't get confused. She also helps us make decisions and move forward in our lives. Debbie Sue is practical and outcome-oriented. For her, everything has a solution, and "thar's no use frettin' 'bout it."

She plays with Edward, four years old now, who for once isn't fighting about eating dinner. He is laughing, gulping down everything on his plate, and asking for more. Debbie Sue hugs Alex and listens to him lament about the stress of third grade.

Debbie Sue is rational and realistic. She is the mother I need most as an adolescent. She gives us boundaries and rules. She demonstrates to me that women can be powerful—knowing who they are and what they want. She shows me that who I am matters because she always looks me straight in the eyes when she talks to me and listens carefully to what I am saying.

Debbie Sue is not afraid to take up space. My whole body relaxes for the hour or two she is with us. She is the steadfast island in the midst of our storm. She is also one of the less frequently seen alters. I don't know if she was created to keep Debby safe or to keep us kids safe. I never see Debbie Sue Out for more than an hour or two, and I can count on two hands the total number of times she's been Out in my life. I also don't recall her coming Out around people other than our immediate family.

My brothers and I believed that she was an alter who was passed down to Debby by our grandmother Tracy because Debbie Sue looks and talks like Tracy. There are other alters who agreed with us.

Maybe this is true, or maybe we are all just a part of Debby's delusional world.

CHAPTER SIXTEEN
TWO

It was May of 1992, the end of my freshman year in college, and John had recently moved out. One day, his stuff was just gone. We didn't ask why, nor was it explained to us.

The year before, I managed to get accepted to a liberal arts college in the Midwest. This was no small feat on my part, considering the limited time I had for working on my college applications and for having to pay all the college application fees myself. I was accepted to five colleges, wait-listed for one, and not accepted to one. The college I chose is the one my aunt told me she had wanted to go to for undergrad and is a well-known Quaker school. I received a scholarship to cover almost all tuition, room, and board fees during my freshman year. Certificates of deposit bought when I was a baby by my grandmother Tracy covered the rest.

In what feels like a miracle carved out of our chaos, some version of the collective known as Debby manifested for three consecutive days of lucidity to drive me to visit the college. The logistics of this feat remain a blur: who watched my brothers, how she negotiated time off work, whether Dad even noticed our absence. These details dissolve in the mist of memory, overshadowed by the sheer wonder of having Debby present, focused, and invested in my future for three whole days.

The eight-hour drive represents more than just distance—it's a journey across generational fault lines. Behind us: my father's abandoned first semester of college, his potential drowning in liquor; Debby's false start and eventual completion through correspondence courses, stealing moments of study between personality shifts. Ahead of us: my chance to break this pattern of interrupted dreams.

College wasn't my escape route, though God knows our family provided plenty to escape from. Instead, it was simply the next expected step in my suburban trajectory, as natural as learning to drive or getting a summer job. In my high school's middle-class ecosystem, where 96 percent of graduates marched off to higher education, college wasn't a question of *if* but *how*. The real miracle wasn't my ambition to go—it was the brief alignment of stars that allowed Debby to be present enough to help me get there.

Anna was Out for a lot of that trip. Other than to help with the driving, I'm not sure why. She never talked with me about college. Debbie Sue popped Out once at a diner to order her favorite foods at breakfast time. None of the depressed or suicidal alters came Out though.

I remember watching Debby navigate the interstate, her hands steady on the wheel, wondering which personality had decided this journey was important enough to maintain focus for three consecutive days. The financial and logistical mountains ahead of us seemed as distant as the horizon—problems for another day. In that moment, I had something rarer than college acceptance: I had Debby, singular and focused, investing in my future.

I returned home multiple times during my first year of college to fill in the gaps when Debby was hospitalized and unable to care for the boys. I had an old Volkswagen that I bought during high school so I could make the trips as needed.

I came home at the end of my first year of college to find Debby curled up in a ball on the living room rug, catatonic and unable to communicate. She didn't seem to know how to move her own body and seemed unable to speak. But she was breathing and didn't appear to be in physical distress. When I shook her awake, she opened her eyes briefly before shutting them again. I had just met the alter Two.

Two is the one who holds the memory of Tracy molesting her when she is two years old. Tracy has Debby pinned down on the upstairs guest room bed in my grandparents' house—the same bed where Tracy molested me. It's covered with a green, thin, wale corduroy bedspread. My grandmother is gripping a bright pink cigarette holder with little rhinestones on it. Tracy, who seems to be disconnected from herself, inserts the holder into Debby's vagina, over and over again, while Debby bleeds and screams. The bleeding eventually brings Tracy out of her dissociated state, and she ends the rape.

According to Alex, Two's been like this for most of the day. This is before cell phones, so he has no way to get ahold of me and alert me of this change while I'm driving the 500 miles from college to home.

This is a different scene from the home-cooked meal around the kitchen table that I imagined coming home to at the end of my long drive. Once again, my role quickly becomes that of rescuer, trying to ensure everyone else gets their basic needs met.

Alex helps me get Two into the car. She still isn't talking and closes her eyes again as soon as I buckle her into the passenger seat.

I run back inside and tell Alex that he is in charge of Edward. Even though they're only ten and six, I have no choice other than leaving them alone while I take care of this alter. I tell Alex I'm sorry, but I know he's a big boy and that he will be okay for an hour or two and to lock the door behind me and not leave the house.

I drive Two the few miles to the psychiatric institution near our house. She remains curled up beside me, not making any noise. There, orderlies get her out of the car. I follow them through the beige and yellow corridor to the main nurses' desk for the adult wing of the institute.

The corridor's wallpaper is arrestingly familiar.

There are a few matching seats with blue cushions along the wall with a clear view of the nurses' desk. I sit there, where I have sat many times before. I lean back and rest my head against the buttress of the wall.

I watch the orderlies carry Two into a padded room, on the other side of the lobby from where I sit. There is a small window in the door to the padded room. After a few minutes, I peek in and see 24 curled in a corner, with her wrists tied so she can't hurt herself. I know it's 24 by the way she has propped her body against the wall and because she isn't resisting being tied up or locked up. She is always noncombative.

An hour passes, and no one has checked in with me. I don't know if I'm supposed to fill out paperwork or speak with the doctor on call, so I finally approach the nurse behind the desk.

The nurse tells me to go home. I guess Debby has been a patient in this hospital enough times that they have everything they need to admit her on a Sunday night. I know I'll have to call the insurance company in the morning, and Debby's boss, and explain to them, yet again, that she needs this hospitalization.

I drive home, round up my brothers, and hug them. I then run down to the basement to start a load of laundry before heading back up to the kitchen to scrounge the refrigerator for dinner.

It's 8:00 p.m. There's nothing in the fridge. The boys have school tomorrow. I'm also starting a new job tomorrow, forty-five minutes away. I have to be at work at 8:00 a.m., the same time the boys have to be at school.

I run to the grocery, using up $50 of the $100 I have to get by on until I get my first paycheck in two weeks. I get enough food to feed us, hopefully, for four or five days. Back home, I make macaroni and cheese for dinner and prepare our sack lunches for the next day, being sure to include handwritten notes on Alex's and Edward's napkins telling them that I love them and I am proud of them.

I help Edward with his first-grade math homework between washing and folding four loads of laundry. I get him to take a bath without too much resistance and tuck him into bed at 10:00—a little late for a kid his age, but not bad considering the day I've had.

Alex wants to stay up and talk to me about Debby. At ten, he's carrying questions too heavy for his age. His eyes hold that familiar hunger for understanding—why our mother fragments into pieces, why our father drowns in alcohol, why our family doesn't work like others do. He wants to dissect Debby's latest crisis as if analyzing it might somehow make it hurt less.

I hug him, breathing in the scent of childhood that still clings to him despite his premature wisdom. The drive home from college has drained my last reserves, and tomorrow's new job looms like a mountain I'll have to climb before sunrise. My heart splinters as I send him to bed—I recognize the need in his eyes, that desperate reach for connection, for answers, for the sister who's always been his second mother. But tonight, I'm running on empty, my emotional fuel gauge hovering below zero. Debby's illness has consumed me like a fire eating oxygen, leaving nothing but ashes of energy.

After Alex's reluctant retreat, I lock the front door with ritualistic precision, finding bitter comfort in the knowledge that tonight's threats, at least, will have to come from outside our walls. A shower washes away college and highway dust but can't rinse off the weight of responsibility. I collapse onto my bed at midnight, setting my alarm for 5:00 a.m.—a mere five hours before I must orchestrate our morning symphony: breakfast to prepare, boys to dress, luggage to unpack, work clothes to iron, all before our 7:00 a.m. exodus.

My exhaustion is so complete that it leaves no room for worry about Debby's well-being. In this moment, her stability or instability exists in a parallel universe—one I'm too tired to visit. Tomorrow will bring its own crises to manage, its own personalities to navigate, but for these few precious hours, I give myself permission to sink into oblivion, letting the weight of being everyone's lifeline slip briefly from my shoulders.

CHAPTER SEVENTEEN

FRANK

A few days after I admitted Debby to the psychiatric institution, I was at my maternal grandfather's house, sitting in the living room where I had sat a hundred times.

I heard the ice tinkle in my grandfather's cocktail glass. It was 5:02 p.m., and Frank was already several sips into his daily communion of Glenlivet and water on the rocks, consumed alongside a small bowl of Planters roasted peanuts.

Frank's entire day revolved around this 5:00 p.m. ritual. Consuming his liquid sacrament of choice was the only thing I consistently recall him doing in my childhood.

I explained to Frank and his second wife, Liz, that yes, Debby does still have multiple personality disorder, and yes, she is suicidal again. The ice in the glass clinks again as Frank takes another sip.

He finally says, "How about that," his go-to response for everything related to our family. This is the irony of his being an award-winning journalist and retired editor of a leading weekly news magazine, where he spent four decades writing and editing hundreds of thousands of words for people to read worldwide. When it comes to our family, Frank's vocabulary shrinks to three words. All neutral words at that. Indiscernible. He can be violently angry, or happy, or oblivious, or downright bored. We never know, because his response is always the same. How about that.

Frank gets up and walks across the living room, through the dining room, to the peach-colored sunroom with the sliding glass doors and the glass ceiling with its own remote-controlled cover for when it rains or snows. I watch him stand at the eight-foot-long bar, fixing himself another drink. There's a mirrored backsplash behind the bar counter, so even though he has his back to me, I can see his face and know he disapproves of what I am telling him.

Frank thinks he's hiding his disapproval.

Everything about Frank was hidden. I'm not sure if he ever knew himself or if being held prisoner during World War II destroyed his sense of self. He survived four amphibious landings before being captured and placed in an officers' prisoner of war (POW) camp in Poland for two and a half years. He and another soldier finally escaped the camp and then spent a year in hiding, making their way slowly from Poland to Greece, where American soldiers finally evacuated them. If Frank wasn't originally a shell of a person, the war turned him into one.

My grandfather liked everything to match the veneer of his shell: his home, his career, his record in the military, and his family. He placed a superficial value on that which is well-packaged.

My presence tainted Frank's world. But of the four alcoholic and mentally unstable and/or inaccessible grandparents I had to choose from, Frank was my favorite. He never once tried to hurt me. Also, he and Liz drove me from DC to Indiana to start my freshman year in college. He only stayed on campus for four minutes after getting my bags out of the trunk of his beige Oldsmobile, but still, it means something to me that he cared enough to take me to school.

It told me that on some level he must love me.

Liz took this moment to confide in me that she had refinished the living room couch and asked if I liked the fabric. I didn't. It was unremarkable.

Liz systemically destroyed all evidence of my grandmother's interior design of the house. Redoing the living room couch was the final nail in the coffin of Tracy's identity. This was Liz's right. She was Frank's wife. And this is her house now.

Most of me doesn't care what she's done, except that in Debby's old bedroom there is a small wooden cabinet where a 1950s Barbie doll lived, complete with several sets of clothes, shoes, hats, and purses. The cabinet is just large enough to hold Barbie and all of her accoutrements, and I wonder if it was built just for her. The Barbie belonged to Debby, and my grandmother saved her for me.

As a child, I found Barbie mesmerizing. I loved her teeny-tiny pink high-heeled shoes, wide sunglasses that actually fit over her ears, the little white purse with the handle draped from her dainty wrist, and the black-and-white bathing suit that looked like zebra skin.

I wasn't allowed toys such as this, so even into my adolescence I would sneak off into the downstairs bedroom, now Frank's office, to hold the Barbie doll and observe how pristine she still was.

Holding the Barbie doll made me feel special. I always knew that while I was playing with her, I was safe.

I wonder if Debby felt the same way when she was little.

I had not yet remembered Tracy sexually abusing me. So for that moment she was just my grandmother, who loved me enough to buy certificates of deposit when I was born to help pay for my college education and saved a Barbie doll for me to play with.

Timing is everything.

The last time I looked, the Barbie was gone.

I know Liz got rid of her without telling me. I resent Liz for taking her away from me. I allow myself to feel angry and childish about this. It feels good to be able to put my anger somewhere.

It is now close to 5:30. I know that by 5:45 Frank and Liz will be in the car, headed to the country club down the road for dinner, where they eat almost every night because Liz hates to cook and my grandfather doesn't know how to.

My grandfather lives by the religion of deadlines, treating them as universal salvation for all of life's messiness. So Frank and Liz rush to meet their self-imposed dinner "deadline" at the club—a meaningless construct given there's no reservation to honor, no companions to meet, no line to navigate. It's theater of urgency performed for an audience of none.

During the infrequent times I accompany them to the club, the scene unfolds with the precision of a well-worn play, each actor hitting their marks with unconscious accuracy. We proceed to our designated table—the same one that's witnessed countless iterations of this performance—like aristocracy claiming their hereditary throne. The waiter, a familiar face in this recurring dream, materializes right on cue.

I order my usual: a garden salad with grilled chicken, adorned with blue cheese and dates. Frank's reaction arrives with clockwork predictability, his face arranging itself into practiced astonishment: "Oh my, what is that?!" His performance of surprise at this familiar dish would be comic if it weren't so telling—a man so committed to maintaining appearances that he's willing to forget the same meal he's questioned dozens of times before.

But tonight I'm not accompanying them to the club. My anxiety is riding high, knowing that I have to ask something of my grandfather.

The list of conversational land mines grows longer with each visit to their house: money (though tonight they will dine at an exclusive club), depression (though it runs in our bloodline), mental illness (though it fragments our family tree), problems (though they multiply like shadows), sadness (though it seeps through our foundations), frustration (though it colors our every interaction), and anxiety (though it's our family's constant companion). These forbidden topics pile up like unopened bills, while time—the one deadline we can't negotiate—runs through my fingers like sand.

I gathered my courage like loose change, knowing that some conversations can't wait for perfect moments. In this cathedral of careful appearances, where even salad ingredients merit theatrical shock, I was running out of time to ask Frank for support.

There is a fifteen-minute window to explain that there is no money to buy groceries for the boys and me and I can't access any of Debby's money because my name isn't on her checking account or credit card.

I tell them what little I know about how long Debby will be in the hospital this time. Her doctor still hasn't called me back. I say we need more groceries, and I won't get a paycheck from my new job for another ten days. In my mind, I am crying out for my grandfather to rescue me and my brothers from this crazy reality we are living in.

Frank's solution to the problem of no food is to feed me for the evening. He invites me to join them for dinner this evening at the club. I explain that I have to get home to my brothers. My grandfather replies, "How about that."

He finally walks down the hall to his office. I hear typewriter keys clacking, and I know he has fed a check into the roller to type out my name and the dollar amount he deems appropriate. This is the typewriter where everything in Frank's life happens: all bills are paid, all stories are told, all resolutions are made, and deadlines are always met.

On the wall above the typewriter was a framed image of Frank on the cover of the weekly news magazine he wrote for, interviewing someone in China—his retirement gift for his decades of service. Next to that, a box-style picture frame with a green felt background, showcasing three medals of honor from the military—a Silver Star, a Bronze Star, and a Purple Heart. There were no photos of his family in his office.

A few minutes later, Frank comes back up the hall, steps into the foyer next to the living room, and hands me a sealed envelope with my name on it, handwritten in his slanted print.

I know better than to open the envelope in his presence to see how much the check is for. Instead, I thank him and glance at my watch. It's 5:44 p.m. I excuse myself because I can see Liz gathering her purse and Frank reaching for his blue suit jacket—the one he always wears to the club on weeknights—in the foyer closet.

It is not comforting to hug my grandfather goodbye. I open the envelope in my car. The check is written out for $100.

CHAPTER EIGHTEEN
DEFIANCE

Going to college was a generous gift for me, originally made possible by the college and by Tracy. I received a substantial scholarship for my freshman year—a recognition of the strength it took to survive my unusual childhood. In the essay I included with my college application, I shared my journey of raising my brothers while managing a mother with 123 personalities and an alcoholic father who didn't pay child support. I wrote of the importance of education for me and how I wanted to go to a Quaker school as I was drawn to their values of simplicity and truth-telling. In my welcome letter, the director of admissions included a personal note about how excited she was for me to be a part of the college community. I felt welcomed and supported—foreign feelings for someone who had spent her teenage years being everyone else's support system.

The scholarship was revoked when tuition came due for year two, with no explanation given. Losing that scholarship reminded me of the unpredictability I'd grown up with, never knowing which of Debby's alters would appear from one moment to the next.

I scrambled to meet my financial needs myself. Tracy's certificates of deposit provided a few thousand dollars each year, which covered what my freshman scholarship did not. Now faced with paying $15,000 a year sans scholarship, I added extra classes so I could graduate early and managed to shave off one semester to save tuition and boarding costs for my senior year, applying the same strategic thinking to my academic career that I'd developed managing our family's chaos.

My college years were marked not by traditional semesters but by episodes with Debby. Each crisis, each hospital stay, each new alter became the real calendar by which I measured time. As a result, most of my college experience was a blur—brief interludes of academic learning and having peers, overshadowed by 1,000-mile round-trip journeys home when Debby had yet another crisis, or a new alter appeared, or when she was institutionalized again. Yet between these familial earthquakes, I discovered unexpected sanctuaries in unlikely places.

I fell deeply in love with the written word in my freshman humanities classes. The process of analyzing texts came naturally to me—after all, I'd spent my childhood reading between the lines, interpreting the subtle shifts in personality that signaled which of Debby's alters had taken control. This keen awareness, born of survival, transformed into an academic strength. I could dissect a text's hidden meanings, unpack layers of symbolism, and articulate complex interpretations with an insight that surprised my professors. Writing became both escape and empowerment, a way to make sense of my fractured narrative through understanding others'.

Junior year brought an unexpected confrontation in my psychology class. The professor, with the certainty of someone who'd only encountered multiple personality disorder in textbooks, dismissed it as controversial and possibly fabricated. I raised my hand, defiance burning in my throat as I challenged his academic theories with lived experience. How could I not defend the reality of a condition I'd witnessed since childhood? The argument that ensued became a turning point—the first time I publicly owned my family's truth without shame, using academic language to validate what I'd always known in my bones.

The rarity of receiving anything from Debby while I was in college made even small gestures monumental. During my final semester in college, she managed to mail me a set of small cooking knives as a birthday present. The gift itself was practical as I was living off campus and needed kitchen tools, but the fact that one of her personalities had maintained enough focus to select, purchase, and mail them felt like a minor miracle. I kept those knives long after their edges dulled, tangible proof that somewhere in the maze of her personalities, my mother remembered me.

These moments of normalcy were precious precisely because they were so rare. Each small victory—mastering literary analysis, standing up to a professor, receiving a birthday gift—felt like an act of defiance against the chaos that defined my family life. I was building an identity separate from being Debby's daughter and my brothers' caretaker, even as those roles continued to shape my college experience.

I lived in a one-level row house in the final semester of my senior year, sharing it with five other women also in their senior year. The house was on a street of matching rental houses, built off campus for upperclassmen. The walls were paper thin, the ceilings low, the rooms tiny, and dishes were always piled up in the teeny kitchen sink. The only redeeming quality was the living room, which had sunlight streaming into it for most of the day—a metaphorical and literal brightness after years of navigating the shadows of my family's mental illness.

I loved living there. It felt so adult to be out on my own, away from the college campus, and to have my best friend, Melissa, living in the room next to mine. There was also mental illness in her family, so she understood living in a delusional world without my having to explain it. She didn't flinch when I mentioned Debby's alters or my brothers' needs—she got it in a way few others could.

Melissa and I cooked meals together, worried about money together, took classes for our human development and social relations major together, and conspired to get our other roommates to "adult," just like we had had to figure out years ago in order to manage our families.

One night we take all of our roommate Cathleen's dirty dishes out of the sink and pile them up on a chair we placed in front of the refrigerator, knowing good and well that Cathleen will stumble into the kitchen at 2:00 a.m., hungry from staying in the computer lab late into the night to finish a paper, and won't be able open the fridge without being confronted with her two weeks of unwashed dishes.

We think it is a hysterical and creative prank. For once, I get to be mischievous instead of responsible—a taste of the normal college experience I largely missed because of my frequent trips home. These moments of playful rebellion feel like healing, like reclaiming pieces of the childhood I'd sacrificed.

Cathleen is not amused. She stubs her toe on the chair, waking us up with her hot temper, and then proceeds to yell at Melissa for a good thirty minutes about how inconsiderate we are. Apparently, her peace and global studies major has not taught her anything useful about the practicalities of conflict resolution or adulthood. I hear every word through the thin walls as I hide under my covers, unable to face one more person in my life not taking responsibility for themselves. After years of managing Debby's personalities and my brothers' needs, others' inabilities to handle basic adult responsibilities triggers a deep exhaustion in me.

The dishes remained unwashed, a small act of defiance against my ingrained role as the responsible one.

PART 5

RECOVERY

(1995–1998)

CHAPTER NINETEEN
RUTH

Ruth, my father's mother, calls me in the early spring of my senior year. Given her ironclad rule that I should call her because "That's what a good granddaughter does," the call catches me off guard.

Ruth is a tiny force of nature, five feet, two inches on her best day, with most of her weight distributed like a top-heavy ship across her chest. I often wonder if physics alone will topple her, though I suspect her iron will would prevent such an undignified fall.

As a former Army major married to a colonel, Ruth approaches life like a military campaign, with rigid protocols for everything from loading a dishwasher to breathing. These rules are never explained, only enforced through a barrage of corrections:

Me, driving exactly at the speed limit in her car: "You're driving too fast!"

Me, signaling and turning right on green: "You should have stopped and looked both ways!"

Me, perfectly centered in a parking space: "You're too close to the car next to us!"

Her criticism is as predictable as artillery fire, each complaint landing with practiced precision.

I dislike Ruth.

Yet there's one memory I cling to. I'm three years old, and there's thunder cracking over the Chesapeake Bay in Eastern Maryland, laid out in front of us in a vast expanse of shimmering obsidian. Ruth is wearing blue polyester pants and a white knit top, her thick white curls corralled by a blue handkerchief tied atop her head like a crown. Her ample bosom becomes my sanctuary as she explains the science of storms, making the frightening familiar. That night, nestled against her on her screened-in porch, I felt safe. In this single memory, I can love my grandmother.

I returned to this moment repeatedly when chaos erupted—during Dad's violent episodes, when Debby cycled through personalities like a deck of cards, when Bryce overdosed, when poverty gnawed at our doors. That night on her lap became my emotional North Star.

Just home from another exhausting sixteen-hour round-trip drive between Indiana and DC—another crisis with Debby, another psychiatric admission, this time to the Psychiatric Institute of Washington's specialized multiple personality disorder wing—I was sitting in my college house's living room when Ruth called. Spring sunlight warmed my feet as Ruth's voice traveled through the phone line, bypassing pleasantries for proclamations: "You are the executor of my estate. I won't allow your father to have anything to do with my money."

No "How are you?" No "Congratulations on graduating!" No acknowledgment of the childhood I sacrificed.

"Your father can't keep a job," she continues, her voice sharp with judgment. "He's always asking for money. He needs to grow up and take responsibility."

The irony of her words isn't lost on me. While Debby fragments into multiple personalities, Ruth remains singularly rigid, wielding money the way Tracy wielded abuse—as a tool for control. At barely twenty-one, I'm being assigned another role of responsibility, another weight to carry.

"I don't want to do that," I protest. "I shouldn't have to do that. I'm not old enough." But Ruth has already changed her will and named me executor, just as my childhood had been altered without my consent.

What I didn't know then was that Ruth was dying of skin cancer. Months later, after graduation, I visited her in the naval hospital with Alex and Edward. We stopped first at her beloved Chesapeake Bay beach, where we collected shells to make her a necklace. When we arrived, she was unconscious. I draped the shell necklace around her neck, a final offering of love. When we returned the next morning, the necklace was gone.

With Ruth, love never stuck.

She died in 1995, two months after my graduation. We scattered her ashes in the Chesapeake Bay, our family's underwater graveyard, where our grandfather Don Sr.'s ashes also rest. I inherited not just her estate but another round of responsibilities: cremation arrangements, memorial planning, house clearance—all while managing a small DC bakery ninety minutes away. The house had to be sold quickly; Ruth didn't leave enough money for basic utilities to be paid for more than a few months.

Once again, I became the good girl, setting aside my own healing to handle another family member's loose ends. My own trauma recovery waited in the wings while I executed Ruth's final orders and tended to Debby after she was discharged, "integrated" at last, from the Psychiatric Institute, in early 1996.

The Bay claims Ruth's ashes like it claimed my grandfather's, while I remain on shore, collecting responsibilities like shells, adding them to an already overflowing basket of family obligations.

CHAPTER TWENTY
DEBBY 2

In the 1980s and '90s, the therapeutic goal for someone with two or more personalities was integration.

I was not a fan of integration, because by 1996 there was a stranger inhabiting our mother's body. We named her Debby 2.

Debby 2 appeared at the tail end of nearly a decade of the collective known as Debby experiencing catatonic depression and moving in and out of psychiatric institutions for suicidal ideation and mental illness. I believe this alter emerged in response to the years of trauma that ensued after Tracy died and Debby attempted suicide. Debby 2 was the collective's attempt at recovery—a personality that lacked emotion but conveniently looked like a mother, spoke like a mother, and answered the questions right. She was their way of continuing to exist in a world that was too much for any of them individually.

Most of the alters disappeared in Debby 2's wake, and we were left to mourn without death certificates or funerals. My brothers and I especially missed Anna, Five, and Debbie Sue. Their presence helped us to feel safe. Debby 2 was a stranger and unknown.

Debby 2 was the alter who frightened me the most because she was void of emotion and continually rewrote history to suit her. She presented as the "integrated" version of Debby, the personality that *should* represent healing. Except this "integrated" version had erased the horror, as if the other 122 personalities never existed, as if my childhood wasn't spent managing their rotating appearances.

Of all of the alters, Debby 2 holds the most memories. She can even recollect stories I only have fleeting glimpses of in my mind's eye—moments I had to fragment myself to survive. On the surface, Debby 2 looks like Debby has recovered from all of her trauma, but this facade of wellness is perhaps the most dangerous personality of all.

Hearing her recite a family story makes my skin crawl. All of the nonemotional details are there, preserved like specimens in formaldehyde. As she is telling the tale, I can picture the exact location, what time of the year it was, what the air felt like on my skin, the taste and smell of the dinner as we were eating it—food I haven't eaten in years. The details are perfect, like a photograph of a crime scene that captures everything except the violence that occurred there.

But the difference between Debby 2 and the other alters is that she has no emotional landscape. While Ten rages with dragon eyes, Five plays like the child Debby never got to be, and Debbie Sue roars with laughter, Debby 2 exists in an emotional vacuum. She can't recall how she was feeling or how any of us were reacting emotionally to that dinner, that pivotal family moment, that catastrophic situation. She's like a security camera that records everything but understands nothing.

She glosses over horrors and replaces them with "facts" that make her look like a dutiful mother and wife. She has no bandwidth to feel what we were feeling or acknowledge the chaos of our reality, the daily navigation of multiple personalities, alcoholic rages, and children trying to raise themselves.

It's as if she has read a casework file about our family and can regurgitate its clinical contents, much like I would later do as a trauma chaplain, except I never forgot the humanity behind the horror. When Debby 2 recites family stories, the hair on the back of my neck stands at attention. An alien has infiltrated our family, wearing my mother's face but empty of her complexity.

Debby 2 conveniently "forgets" any memory in which she may have caused harm to our family because it doesn't fit in her narrative. The focus must always be on her as either victim or heroine of both her story and our family's. Being around her makes me nauseous and has me questioning my sanity, especially when she just stares at me blankly if I attempt to contradict her historical rewrites. Her emotional void is perhaps the most violent of all Debby's personalities—not because of what it does but because of what it erases.

On the flip side, Debby 2 is consistently functional. She has found a way to survive. She works until she's sixty-seven, owns her own home, volunteers, gets involved in political issues, goes to church, shows up for her grandkids, and pays her taxes. She is an all-around good, liberal, middle-class American.

I cannot stand her.

I want to be a child who is loved and cared for and adored. Even with her integration and survival and functionality, Debby 2 is incapable of offering that to me.

CHAPTER TWENTY-ONE

DON

The call about my father's death comes on a sunny afternoon while I'm checking messages on my home answering machine. Sitting alone in my office, I'm trying to breathe between meetings. It's 1998, and I'm just a few years into my career. At age twenty-four, I am in the most prominent position I have ever held. Managing a large team, I'm putting together a brand-new, week-long international arts festival to take place on the National Mall in Washington, DC. I dreamed the festival into existence and built it from the ground up in my mind, channeling the same organizational skills I'd developed coordinating my brothers' lives while tracking Debby's rotating alters. I hire staff and vendors and work with my team to bring together children and their parents from nearly seventy countries to attend the event.

I minored in arts administration in college because of my love of the arts, which Dad cultivated in me at an early age. In fact, along with another student, we created that minor for the college because we both knew we wanted to work in the arts. I had my first job at an arts organization within a year of graduating from college, and I advanced quickly.

I return the call from a deputy sheriff. He introduces himself, tells me he is from the town where my father lives, and asks how I am related to Donald Churchman. I don't want to answer. I'm already irritated, my body remembering years of his alcoholic rages and of protecting my brothers. "I'm his daughter," I say haughtily. "What is he in jail for this time?"—the weary question of a child who grew up managing her father's chaos.

He told me my father was dead. I knew I was supposed to feel sad, but I went numb—the same protective numbness that helped me survive my role as family anchor. The deputy told me that someone would call me soon with more information. Unable to breathe, I hung up the phone.

It rang again less than five minutes later. I hadn't moved. I picked up the handset and nervously wrapped the cord around my fingers—a gesture reminiscent of how I used to ground myself during Debby's personality switches.

"Ma'am, I'm so sorry for your loss. Can you tell us please what you would like us to do with your father's body?" I say I don't know and ask why I have to make the decision. This time I am speaking to the sheriff of the small town where my father lived. The sheriff stutters, unsure what to say. He seems nervous, or distraught, or both. He resolves this by becoming even more professional, reminding me of how I learned to manage crisis at fourteen, becoming the composed one while adults fell apart around me. "Um... He listed you as next of kin, ma'am. What... what... what do you want us to do?"

Once again, I was thrust into the role of responsible one, managing another family crisis. Even in death, my father found a way to make me parent him. The sunny afternoon felt suddenly cold, as if all the years of being the family's anchor were casting their shadow over this moment.

Apparently Dad had been dead for several days, and a decision about embalming his body versus cremation needed to be made immediately. Cremation seemed like the easiest decision to make as it was a tradition in our family. The sheriff told me he would inform the only funeral home in town of my decision.

"But how did he die?" I finally think to ask. The stuttering reappears. "Well, uh, it seems he's been dead for several days, ma'am. Um... His landlord found him dead in his apartment. We think it was a suicide."

The sheriff decided that I would meet him in my father's small town in Maryland the next day, deal with my father's apartment, and go to the funeral home to sign paperwork.

I called my roommate, who worked just one block away from my office. We've known each other since seventh grade, and I trusted her with this information. I couldn't move from my office chair. She arrived in less than ten minutes. My body wouldn't cooperate. She lifted me up, linked arms with me, and got me back home to our teeny townhouse in southwest DC.

I threw up when I got home, when I realized I was exactly the same age—twenty-four—that my parents were when they had me. When they were twenty-four, they were experiencing new life and becoming parents for the first time. For me, my twenty-fourth year will forever be marked by my father intentionally ending his life. I don't want this memory. I don't want this life. I don't want to be associated with this kind of death. My embarrassment matched my anger.

Trying to figure out how to tell Debby that the man she had been married to for twenty-one years was dead felt virtually impossible. That night I took the Metro to her house in Northern Virginia. I took her upstairs to her bedroom and shut the door. We sat on the familiar white popcorn bedspread that had covered her bed for the past twenty years.

"There's something really hard I have to tell you, Mom." I try to sound empathetic. I'm sure she thinks I am pregnant or have lost my job. Instead I tell her fact for fact about my afternoon.

"I got a call from a sheriff in the town where Dad lives. He called with bad news. He told me that Dad died. He said I needed to figure out what to do and that I am responsible." I leave out the part about him ending his own life because I don't have proof yet that it happened that way.

Then I cry, and Debby 1 comes Out and holds me. With her arms wrapped around me, my body heaves in sobs, finally releasing me from the state of shock I've been in for hours.

"Oh, sweetie, this must be so hard for you. I'm so sorry that you got the call. You must be so upset."

This is complicated grief. I have lost a father. She has lost a man she was married to for decades but intentionally divorced. I flittingly wonder what kind of grief is appropriate for a divorced woman.

I am surprised in that moment that Debby 1 is able to be Out and present with me. I haven't seen her in a decade. I am thankful for the unexpected gift of time with her. She is always nice to me.

Alex and Edward, both now adolescents, are still living at home with Debby. Bryce has been homeless since he dropped out of high school five years ago, but he has a cell phone, so we are able to get ahold of him if needed. We sit Alex and Edward down on the living room sofa to tell them what I know about Dad.

I tell them that Dad's landlord found him. I leave out the part about his dead body stinking up the second floor of his apartment building. I don't mention his landlord throwing up from the stench. I don't share how upset the sheriff was on the phone earlier that afternoon.

Hugging my brothers, I tell them how sorry I am and that I love them very much. We call Bryce and tell him. Then we sit for a long time in the living room, with Debby 1 trying to convince us to have a memorial and all of us responding that we don't need closure.

24, who has been divorced from Dad for a decade at this point, announces she is going with me to meet the sheriff to offer "support." Of course she is now Out—in her always steadfast commitment to death. Here is her opportunity to once again be close to it. She is drawn like a moth to the flame of Dad's death.

24's immediate river of tears indicates that I will instead be supporting her. Her tears match my anger, and her sadness is creeping its way into my stoicism.

The next day, the sheriff greets us outside of his office in a tiny town in rural Maryland, population 501. He is about six feet, five inches and easily 350 pounds.

24, the sheriff, and I cram into his 5' x 8' office, along with his giant desk and three rickety, mismatched chairs. When we sit down, our knees touch. After a moment the sheriff breaks down in tears. 24 joins him.

I hand them both tissues. I am numb, without affect.

The sheriff tells us that he lost his wife six months ago to cancer. He appears profoundly grief-stricken.

"This is just so hard to have to deal with another death so close to my wife dying. My deputies and I have never had to deal with such a gruesome death before."

The sheriff then looks me squarely in the eye and says, "I don't want you to see your father's body. It's too far gone. We identified the body for you."

It was an act of gracious compassion, but it left me wondering if there was any chance it wasn't Dad who died. I was mad that the sheriff didn't think I could handle seeing my father.

The sheriff then offered to take us to Dad's apartment. In the car, I grab 24 by the shoulder and speak in a calm, reasonable voice, masking my anger at her and the situation: "You need to pull it together. This isn't hard only for you." I was counting the minutes until I could be away from her. Her sadness was sucking the life force out of me, and one of us needed to be a functional adult.

I had never been to Dad's apartment. In fact, I had no idea he was even living in Maryland. When I walked into the little studio, which had a mattress on the floor in one corner and a card table and chair in the other, I knew exactly how he had died. I saw the bottle of pills and two bottles of bourbon next to the mattress. There was an outline on the sheets of where his body began decomposing. The leftover stench of rotting flesh made me gag, although the sheriff had thought to open the windows before we arrived.

The week prior I intuited that something was wrong with Dad. Even though I told him clearly when I left for college that I didn't want to have a relationship with him, he still called every year on my birthday and left a message. I secretly counted on those calls to remind me that there was a part of him that did love me. He hadn't called that year. I remember noticing and wondering. Fear crept in: Had he forgotten the day of my birth, the day he became a parent, or had something happened?

Instead, the person who was supposed to love me most in the world ended his own life a week after my twenty-fourth birthday.

I went back to my father's studio apartment the weekend after meeting with the sheriff, this time taking my brothers. We planned to pick up our father's ashes from the funeral home and go through his belongings, in case my brothers wished to keep any of his possessions. The landlord told me he would handle the rest. Dutifully, I grabbed all of Dad's papers, thinking that as his executrix—which I was, by default, as his next of kin—I would look through them to see if he owed any debts or had any accounts to close.

On the papers, Dad had written poems, haiku, grocery lists, stories, and random phone numbers. A garbage bag full came home with me, and my roommate and I went through it.

I discovered, unexpectedly, almost brutally, that my father was a deeply spiritual man. My understanding of him changed when I began to read his poetry.

He is no longer just memories of anger and violence. His poetry reminds me that he was not simply the one-dimensional, abusive man I most often remembered him as.

I am the plow that tills my field.
I am the mule which pulls it.
I am the seed I sow behind.
I am the crop which emerges.
And I too am sun and rain;
the fertilizer and puller of weeds.
I the storm and insect plague;
the protector and the vermin.
My life's the land I cultivate,
to blossom or burn at my own rate,
and in the winter to lie fallow,
until spring returns.

I believe my father understood himself as a poisonous snake, full of his mother's controlling, abusive words, his father's passivity, and his lack of "success" in the world. From a very early age, I felt that my father did not like himself. As a child, I had no empathy for him. I had never thought of him as a spiritual person, or as someone who took responsibility for himself.

I refused to deal with my father's death. Taking only one day off work, I approached his death as a test of my management skills and proceeded to manage my family and his estate for the next year while directing the international art project.

The only emotion I emitted about my father's death was anger. The anger that he couldn't find a way to recover after he and Debby divorced built like a disease inside of my body, finally erupting a year later.

CHAPTER TWENTY-TWO
RESURRECTION

Almost a year to the day after Dad's death, I stopped functioning. I got sick and had to quit my job. I went to bed in March and couldn't get out of bed until October. My body refused to cooperate, and I felt like it was betraying me. I had a migraine, which lasted every day for over five months. I spent days in a fever-filled fog, talking to myself, unable to think clearly. My body, mind, and spirit were out of control, and I had no idea what to do.

I eventually got into therapy. I sat in weekly sessions where my therapist said things like, "Punch this pillow to show me how angry you are." I reluctantly pushed the pillow around, thinking the exercise was ridiculous. My anger about my father's death, Debby's mental illness, and my fucked-up childhood was stuck inside of me. I had shoved it down so deeply that I could barely access it.

I can't fully connect to any of my emotions. Anger is the closest to surfacing, so I practice feeling it, with small punches into the pillow during therapy sessions and in daily journaling. My heart remains numb.

Overwhelm, terror, anxiety, grief, betrayal, hostility, even joy and sadness are too far away for me to grasp. I know I'm supposed to feel more things than just anger. I observe friends and colleagues and their myriad emotions, so quick to surface. I watch television programs to see how other people express themselves. I wonder if I'll ever be able to recover myself and function as more than a shell of a person.

My therapist hands me a sheet of paper with different facial expressions and emotions tied to each of those expressions. For the happy face, the emotion is joy. For the face with the gaping mouth, the emotion is surprise. I practice making those faces in the mirror. I quickly learn how to pretend I'm having certain emotions, even though I can't feel them in my body. I assume there is something critically wrong with me, that I feel nothing. I don't tell anyone, even my therapist, about how numb I am. I need her, and other people, to see me as capable, and competent, and not a victim of a lifetime of trauma.

Journeys don't always start with a destination. Sometimes they begin with the simple acknowledgment that things need to be different. That is how resurrection begins. You realize that in the midst of all of the brokenness, all of the grief and heartache and "what ifs," there is an opportunity to resurrect yourself.

In 1999, in the year after Dad died, I began asking myself questions like, "Where is God in this?" "How do I make sense of my upbringing, of the seemingly crazy things that happened in my childhood and to Debby?"

"How do I feel my feelings and inhabit my body?"

"Who am I when I am not just living in response to trauma?"

At age twenty-five, my questions aren't quite this articulate or elegant, but the intention is there, burning like a pilot light that survived years of emotional storms.

I know it is time for me to stop living in reaction to everything around me, and, most importantly, to no longer be captive to Debby. This feels like a spiritual calling, but I don't yet have words to express it.

I know it's time for me to reinvent myself, just like I watched Debby do so many times, with new versions of her popping Out via alternate personalities. But, unlike Debby, I don't feel the need to dissociate in order to move forward and heal. I do feel the need to evolve. I want to learn how to thrive, not just survive. I want to become whole rather than shatter into pieces like my mother did.

Mainly, I show up at my Quaker meeting every Sunday morning and hide in the corner. I sit stiffly erect, my back against the meeting bench, a wall propping me up on one side—the same rigid posture I maintained while managing our family's chaos. Weeping silently for the entire hour, my internal wailing prayer generally goes like this:

"Where the fuck are you, God?"

After six months of therapy, tears, and prayer, I recognize my life has to radically change. But how do I reconstruct myself without a foundation of knowing how to be a whole person? How do I learn integration when my primary model of coping was a mother who split into 123 different selves?

I didn't have language for any of this yet. All I understood was that I could no longer live in reaction to my family. What I couldn't know then was that this journey would eventually lead me to become a trauma chaplain and then a trauma recovery expert, teaching others how to heal from the very kinds of wounds that had shaped my childhood. The questions that began in that Quaker meetinghouse would become the foundation for helping others find their way back to wholeness.

PART 6

RECONSTRUCTION

(2002–2014)

CHAPTER TWENTY-THREE
THE PSYCHIC

I met Adam in 2002.

He shows up at Quaker meeting one day, inadvertently sitting on the Facing Bench (the bench where the elders responsible for opening and closing worship sit). He's tall, with dramatic good looks and an impressive bachelor's degree from Yale University. He begins following me around the meetinghouse for the next few months, hunched over so he doesn't appear to be nearly a foot taller than my diminutive five feet six inches. He wants to participate in whatever activity I am organizing. He sometimes stands on the stairs below me to ask if he can join, so I can look him square in the eye while he asks. Other times, he just shows up.

I am leading the Young Adult Quakers group. This group comprises more than 30 twenty- to forty-year-old Quakers who are mainly working for government or not-for-profit organizations in the DC area. We move around DC and our meetinghouse in packs, wearing jeans and T-shirts with witty political slogans or flannel shirts on top of the T-shirts when the weather turns cool. Most of us roll out of bed on Sunday morning just in time for worship at 10:00 a.m., arriving by bike or the Metro subway system.

Our commonality? We want to change the world for good. Debbie's activist influence has me fitting very well into this community.

Adam is elusive, idealistic, and captivating, with his broad chest, full head of hair, and ten-dollar words. By twenty-seven, he has already made his first million by founding a technology company with a business partner that sold for multimillions only a few years after its launch. He is committed to living simply and has been traveling the world, on his own spiritual journey of sorts. While traveling in the United Kingdom he stumbled across Quakerism (which was founded in England) and began attending Meetings for Worship in England and across Europe. Raised in Baltimore, he moved to DC after college to find work as an engineer. Although he retired at twenty-seven, he finds his way back to DC after his European travels, seeking community.

His first stop is my Quaker meeting.

Adam and I talk about living in intentional community together. We begin sort of dating, but neither of us are particularly good at feeling our feelings or being physically intimate. We are safe for each other in that way. I am drawn like a moth to the flame of his inability to love me.

During this time, Debby 2 meets and marries Joe. They are both members of the same Quaker meeting. Joe, like Debby 2, lacks emotion or really any sense of affect. They are a perfect fit.

I develop a habit of forgetting Joe is in the room when he and Debby 2 live together because he is either hidden behind a newspaper or just watching Debby 2 do all the talking. I think she prefers it that way—he is her constant audience.

Bryce has a girlfriend, a woman he met in Narcotics Anonymous. For once, sobriety seems to be sticking with him. He trained as a plumber's apprentice when he got sober a few years before meeting his girlfriend and now has a job with a steady paycheck. They get pregnant, and marriage seems like the next logical step to take; they do so a few years before Debby 2 and Joe. Their first child is a girl, and they have a son a year or so later. Bryce and his wife buy a small townhouse in the suburbs of Baltimore to raise their family.

Joe was basically a fly on the wall of our family for several years, up until the moment Bryce's daughter, then three, came home from a weekend visit to Debby and Joe's house and announced that Joe touched her vagina.

Bryce called Alex, Edward, and me to relay what his daughter had told him. We were all deeply concerned about his daughter's safety and immediately agreed that she would never stay at Debby's house again and certainly would never be around Joe again.

Debby 2 immediately deflected and rewrote history in her favor, as is her wont. During a phone call to me a few days later, she reported, "Oh no, nothing happened. Joe is harmless. Your brothers and sister-in-law are just overreacting."

Me: "Why would a three-year-old child make up a story about a man touching her vagina?"

Debby 2: "Kids make up stories all of the time. He was probably just helping her get dressed."

Me: "Why weren't you helping her get dressed? She is your grandchild."

Debby 2: "Why are you making such a big deal out of this? I already told you nothing happened."

It was shocking to me that since Debby had been sexually abused at such a young age by her own mother, she would not immediately side with her granddaughter and advocate for her. But I had Debby 2's number. I knew damn good and well that this would be her response to any situation that did not position her as the perfect grandmother and wife and that arguing with her was a losing battle.

We all told her that we no longer wished to interact with Joe. We didn't want to spend holidays with him, we didn't want to go to their house, and he was not welcome in our homes. We set the boundary and refused to budge. It took almost two years, but Debby 2 finally separated from and eventually divorced Joe.

By the time of this incident with Bryce's daughter, I was several years into running a consulting firm with a friend. We were working with arts organizations in the DC metropolitan area, helping them secure corporate funding and organize fundraising events. I launched the business when I was twenty-four, in the year following Dad's death. I had no idea what I was doing as a business owner, but that had never stopped me from taking on a big challenge. Running the consulting firm allowed me to work remotely for extended periods, so it seemed feasible for Adam and me to begin visiting communities across the United States.

I was on one of these visits when I discovered I am psychic.

Maybe I've always been psychic, but so much of my intuitive abilities have been directed for so long toward Debby that I wasn't paying attention to anything else. Tracking her slightest facial and physical changes, her moods, her personalities, and her needs was my full-time job.

In my childhood, Debby's unpredictability, as well as Dad's, presented so much risk to me that I became hyperattuned. Every move they made, or didn't make, had implications for me. I learned to be hyperattentive to anything in my space that could be unsafe.

So maybe I'm psychic, or maybe I'm just more in touch than many people because of my years of trauma. Either way, I was not prepared for what happened during that trip with Adam in the fall of 2003.

Adam and I had an argument, the kind of argument you have when you've been with your partner long enough to viscerally resent their ways of showing up in the world after a long day. It took place in the middle of a country road—a road neither of us was familiar with, having driven it for the first time that afternoon.

Five hours earlier, we had turned off the road onto the long driveway of the hippie commune we were visiting. It was an intentional community that owned four hundred acres in the middle of an otherwise small, conservative Virginia county. It was completely off the grid, meaning it didn't rely on any corporate or government system to function and was solar powered and well fed. The communards grew all their own food, slaughtered their own beef, made tofu and hammocks to produce income, and referred to my hometown of DC as Babylon. They found the notion of this city as the center of the free world hypocritical. For the communards, people who helped to perpetuate systems and structures of oppression were worshipping the wrong idols.

We were immediately greeted by a large and very tall woman named Mellie. She was overly enthusiastic, hugging and kissing Adam on the lips, and she didn't have far to reach because she was nearly as tall. I had never seen nor heard of this woman before. Over the next few minutes, I learned that Mellie had met Adam at some social justice event or protest (I could never keep them all straight) in DC and invited him to visit her. I realized that Mellie had no idea Adam had a girlfriend. It was obvious to me that she was interested in him and deeply disappointed that I was there.

Apparently, Mellie and I are now in a competition for Adam's attention. I'm already irritated with them as we go to dinner together in the communal dining hall. We eat seasoned black beans and rice, green salad with homemade tahini dressing, and vegan macaroni and cheese made with nutritional yeast. For dessert there is apple crisp. Over dinner we hear the communard gossip—who is fighting with whom, and who we should friend or stay away from.

At 10:00 p.m., Adam and I decide to take a walk because, frankly, we are bored. The visit hasn't gone exactly the way we had envisioned it with our idealist late-twenties imaginations. We thought these people were changing the world, not infighting. Granted, we have only been there for five hours, but still, we are frustrated because we haven't yet had a transformational experience.

It is a great night for a walk. At the end of October, it is still remarkably warm, even at that hour in the evening when the cool of the darkness should have settled. My fingers should feel chilly enough to stuff into my pockets. Instead, sweat drips down the small of my back, sticking my lightweight jacket heavily against my body. This is where our fight begins.

I become increasingly convinced that a giant truck is barreling down the road behind us. I sense the driver unknowingly speeding on the seldom-traveled country road in the moonless shadows, listening to the only radio station available in the small county. I picture him singing along to a country western song about a man who lost a girl, played some pool, and then drank himself to death. Isn't that how these songs always go?

As I hear the truck get closer to us, I start shouting at Adam, demanding that we get out of the middle of the road. He says he neither sees nor hears a truck.

I am internally railing against how Adam is being. He has a habit of disbelieving any statement I make that doesn't sound true to him. His impressive height and commanding presence make his dismissals imposing and authoritative. He reminds me of John, Debby's former boyfriend. Both use their height and education to intimidate others. I am irritated at myself for falling for someone so similar to John.

I think to myself that he is an idiot asshole and that I am going to break up with him if he survives the truck smashing his remarkably tall body into the pavement. I know these are not really the best thoughts to have about your boyfriend in the moments before his catastrophic death, but I can't help myself.

In the next instant, I fall to the ground on my knees, unable to move. I feel as if a young woman in her early twenties, with long stringy brown hair and a slight frame, has come into my body. I feel suicidal. I feel crazy. I feel overwhelmed and desperate. I can't breathe or move my limbs. My body is glued to the ground, and time has stopped. I can't find myself inside my body and don't understand where I could have gone and why this woman is inside me.

Doesn't she have her own body?

I feel Adam's arms trying to pull me up in the moonless shadows. But I don't understand what he is doing. I focus on the silence, thinking how lovely it must be to live in a place where it is so quiet at night. So different from the familiar city noises, the incessant post-9/11 fighter jets flying over the US Capitol every hour of the day and night, just a few blocks from my house; the drug deals gone bad, ending in shootings on the other side of my road, the perpetual sound of the ambulance, or the police car, cleaning up the mess; and my new roommate, who doesn't understand just how much noise he makes when he gets home at 2:00 a.m. from the dance club he frequents.

I have found silence in the country, except I can't make my body move. I am cemented to the middle of the road, unable to hear what my boyfriend is saying to me.

Then it all stops.

Shaking and pulling me upright, Adam shouts at me to answer him. Then he just holds me and weeps. It has only been a few minutes between hearing the truck and my body snapping out of its paralysis. It feels like a lifetime and like no time at all has passed.

Adam says there was no truck. No vehicle had come barreling down the road. No young woman had been there. From his perspective, nothing happened, just me falling to my knees, unable to speak or respond.

We don't know what to do, so eventually we walk back to the building where we're staying with Mellie.

It is only out of desperation that I agree to share with Mellie the details of what has just happened. I have surmised that sharing my vulnerable state with her could be used against me. Remarkably, Mellie sits quietly and listens carefully to what I say about this woman who entered my body.

I expect Mellie to tell me I am crazy, dramatic, or just trying to be the center of attention. After all, I had already discerned that Mellie is all of these things, so why wouldn't she project them onto me?

Instead, she softly says, "Oh, that woman sounds like Delancey. She came to our community last year. She was twenty-three and looking for a place to live. We worried about accepting her as a member here because she struggled deeply with depression. She committed suicide last October. We found her body in a truck."

When I asked Mellie where the truck was parked, she replied that it was on the edge of their property, along the same country road we had walked on that night.

That night on the country road opened up my clairvoyance. I now have access to the emotions of the living and dead. But my own emotions still remain elusive.

It is nearly two years before I have another encounter with a spirit of the dead. In the meantime, my relationship with God has developed significantly. I am starting to notice that when I slow down and listen, I am always given guidance.

The guidance, though, is only given one step at a time. It requires that I pay exquisite attention to what God asks of me or invites me into. This guidance is always about returning home to the truth of who I am, without the trauma. My soul self.

As long as I pay attention and move in response to this greater guidance, I am held, carried, and always provided for. This becomes my safety mechanism for operating in the world. This is also how I learn who I am outside of existing in Debby's reality.

This was how it finally became safe to feel my feelings, because I knew that with God carrying me forward, I could let my guard down. My need to self-protect from other people and even my own emotions was no longer necessary. I began to notice that I actually had a lot of feelings. In fact, my feelings came rushing up to the surface so quickly that it became hard for me to determine what I actually wanted because I was always emotional, and my myriad emotions were giving me mixed messages.

So there I was, having all of the feelings, and God was trying to get my attention in order for me to take the next aligned step. I kept saying yes to God despite the confused feelings because with God, the voice was distinct from my emotions.

God is a slow, steady, yet fleeting voice in the center of my forehead, guiding me gently and lovingly forward. Sometimes the guidance comes like a bird striking a window—a sharp, unexpected tap that pulls my attention upward from the swamp of my feelings. The sound reverberates through my awareness, a divine percussion that says, "Look here, beloved. There's more than what you're feeling." In these moments, I'm reminded that alignment with divine purpose doesn't require emotional certainty, only willing surrender to that gentle, knowing touch in the center of my forehead.

My emotions were chaotic, confusing, and ever present. They drowned out my ability to say no to God. I was still unsure how to trust them, but at least I was having them.

In 2004, when I was thirty years old, I went to live and work in a Quaker community and education center outside of Philadelphia, Pennsylvania—alone. The year and a half with Adam had been a master class in emotional whiplash. The closer we became, the more he claimed interest in polyamory, wanting multiple female partners. I couldn't decipher whether his fascination was rooted in fear of intimacy—polyamory serving as a convenient shield against true vulnerability with any one person—or if it was his passive-aggressive exit strategy. Maybe he genuinely believed none of us was designed for monogamy. The uncertainty was maddening.

The part of me that had been abandoned repeatedly by my parents and others was terrified of losing him. I had fallen completely, recklessly in love, and at least once a month I would catch him flirting with other women—each instance a small knife twist to my already fragile sense of worth. I convinced myself that if I just loved him fiercely enough for both of us, he would stop searching for something outside our relationship.

This was my familiar survival strategy, the same one I'd deployed with my family: If I just willed them to stay alive hard enough, maybe they wouldn't die. It had worked, sort of—only Dad had died by suicide. So I applied the same desperate logic to Adam, willing him to love me, to love us. But love cannot be willed into existence, and my efforts only highlighted the emptiness where his commitment should have been.

The opportunity at the Quaker community arrived like divine intervention. A friend forwarded me a job opening, casually asking if I knew anyone who might be interested. Within weeks, I had the position. Leaving Adam in DC felt like stepping off a cliff, but I told myself I had to discover what it meant to deserve better than his inability to truly love me.

Of course, Adam followed me to Philadelphia, occasionally attempting reconciliation with the same push-pull dynamic that had defined our relationship—always approaching the edge of real commitment, never quite able to leap. But by then, surrounded by the quiet wisdom of the Quaker community, I was beginning to understand the difference between someone who wanted to be with me and someone who simply didn't want to lose me.

Once I moved to Philly, I started training for Reiki certification. This was my attempt to learn how to work with my psychic skills. I wanted to create healthy boundaries for myself because of what I was perceiving and feeling about other people. After spending my childhood reading the subtle shifts that signaled which of Debby's alters was emerging, I needed to determine when to turn off this hyperawareness.

Feeling the need to protect myself was so different from how I existed during my teens and twenties. I had no boundaries then. I couldn't afford them when handling our family trauma. I felt overly responsible for everyone, my nervous system trained to anticipate needs before they arose. Managing the train car of alters meant that I was always on high alert—feeling everyone else's feelings so that I could predict violence or trouble. I learned to read the yellow gleam in Ten's dragon eyes, to sense when Five needed to play, to notice when 24's depression took over.

But I knew I had to protect myself first, to put my needs ahead of others. This shift marked the beginning of my own healing journey. The skills I'd developed surviving my childhood—reading energy, anticipating needs, understanding the complexity of trauma—transformed into tools for healing rather than just survival. What once made me a capable manager of the aftermath of Debby's personalities became the foundation for helping others navigate their own trauma recoveries.

In 2005, my friend Amy asked me to come to her house. She heard I was training in Reiki and wanted me to energetically "clear" her basement. She and her husband had lived in the house for twenty-some years, and the basement was their venue for unfinished projects and family remnants. She had been trying for months to sort through the piles of chaos, to clean up and streamline her family's possessions, before having the basement refinished into a mother-in-law apartment.

Although I agree to the clearing, I have essentially no idea what I am doing. Reiki is a form of energy healing that involves using gentle touch to guide energy through the physical body. It's primarily used to promote relaxation and well-being for people but can also be used for spaces. I had only ever done Reiki on people, not places, so I felt intimidated by Amy's request.

In an effort to meet expectations, I bring a smudge stick and my friend Nancy, who is trained in Native American rituals. Nancy always came across like she knew what she was doing. I felt she would compensate for my lack of experience.

We carefully walk through the basement with the lit smudge stick, smoke swelling so thickly we could have fumigated anything, living or dead. The whole time I am wondering if Amy recognizes my ineptitude. She works in a bookstore, lives in the suburbs, and all her dishes match. I am actually astounded that it even occurred to her to ask me to clear the energy from her basement. I never think of myself as having it all together.

About twenty minutes into the process of choking on smoke and feigning competency, I find myself in a wine cellar. I am surprised to see a girl in her early twenties with shoulder length, dirty-blond hair who keeps saying the word "sister." Cognizant enough to recognize that she is a spirit, my heart lurches when I see her. I don't want to see another dead person and definitely don't want her taking over my body like Delancey did. Panicked, I hightail it out of the room and out the basement door into the backyard.

Nancy and Amy follow me, peppering me with questions. Nancy seems displeased with my level of anxiety. She makes small, high-pitched wheezing sounds every time I suggest we not go back inside.

I turn my body away from her.

When I calm down enough, I relay the information about the girl I have seen. Amy immediately starts weeping. The girl, she says, sounds exactly like her sister Emily, who died by suicide when she was twenty-four. This was thirty years ago. Many of Emily's belongings are still in the basement.

Amy wants me to come back inside and talk to Emily. Nancy agrees that this is the best course of action. I think it is a terrible idea because of what happened with Delancey, but I eventually relent because I can sense the importance of this interaction. Returning to the wine cellar, I find that Emily isn't where I had left her. I wait a moment, stilling my body and becoming present to what is around me. A few minutes later, she appears. I ask her what she needs and wants. She expresses a desire to hug Amy.

I still can't really articulate how I knew what this young spirit was expressing to me. Technically, it wasn't verbal communication, but it felt verbal to me, much like I learned to read the subtle shifts between Debby's alters before they fully emerged.

Logistically, I'm not exactly sure how these sisters can hug one another considering that Amy can't see where Emily's spirit is standing. So, I set my anxiety aside and I hug Amy on Emily's behalf, my body once again becoming a vessel for another's needs.

As I wrap my arms around Amy, Emily inhabits my body. It is the exact feeling I had two years previously in my encounter with Delancey on that dark, rural Virginia road. I am in my body but not in my body at the same time, a sensation eerily familiar to watching Debby switch between personalities. Emily is using up most of the space in my body. I am squished to the side, an afterthought. Again, I don't understand how there can be so much room for another person to exist inside me as well, though years of making space for Debby's personalities in my life had perhaps prepared me for this moment.

All of Emily's emotions became my emotions, the sadness and grief for dying before her time, the missed opportunities to grow and mature, the desire for forgiveness from Amy. This emotional absorption felt different from the hypervigilance I developed as a child, more purposeful, more healing.

A few minutes later, and she was gone. Not in the basement or in the wine cellar. Just gone. There was a sense of resolution in my heart. Somehow, I knew that Emily had finally crossed over, thirty years after her death.

Amy wept for a long time, grateful for the opportunity to have been with her sister again. As Amy sobbed, exhaustion seeped into my bones, and gratitude welled up inside me for the opportunity to accompany Amy in this way, to offer this needed resolution. I was glad she was willing to trust me enough to recognize the possibility of her sister being in her basement, waiting decades for a hug.

I told Amy I needed to go home, that I was tired and needed to rest. It had been a big day for all of us, and she understood.

Nancy helped me get back to the car. I sensed she desperately wanted to analyze what had just happened, to discuss what appeared to be a recurring and increasingly awkward theme in my life—the spirits of women who have died by suicide winding their way into my body. She found my abilities fascinating. I found them exhausting. I had no interest in becoming the main character of a made-for-television movie about a woman who feels called to heal the living but instead begins accompanying the dead.

The encounter with Emily coming into my body opened my psychic floodgates further. All of a sudden, I could "see" everything. In living people, I sensed their moods, childhood histories, traumas, desires, and hopes. I began seeing spirits of the dead, angels, and demons. Walking into buildings, I immediately knew who was born and who died in those spaces. Walking in the woods, I sensed hidden burial grounds.

I am a lightning rod for the unseen. My psychic abilities have now grown way beyond anything I could have imagined for myself. I am walking between the worlds of life and death. Another version of me is coming through.

I find it overwhelming to be with anyone else, a group of people, or, heaven forbid, a crowd of people. Everything is overstimulating and too much. When I try to go to new places, I spend most of my time feeling somewhat insane because I never know if the emotions or physical reactions I feel are mine or someone else's.

I had a handle on my abilities with Debby because I was so focused on the alters and managing danger and violence. She was a psychic outlet that I was comfortable with. Now that I have opened my abilities up beyond the confines of our immediate family, I feel like I'm drowning. I don't want to know all of this information about other people.

CHAPTER TWENTY-FOUR
QUAKER SHAMAN

In an attempt to alleviate my feeling of drowning in psychic information, I asked my Reiki teacher for help. She admitted she had no idea how to help me and sent me to an energy healer named Brad. Brad was really good at teaching me how to have healthy boundaries, how to keep the energy of the living and the dead out of my space, and how to clear out my own energy so I could continue to have my own personal experiences.

But Brad couldn't see everything I could see, and eventually his bag of tricks ran out.

Several friends recommended I train with a shaman. I was open to the idea but had no idea how to find someone like that. They didn't exactly list themselves in the yellow pages. But this was also God's guidance for me. I knew because of what happened next.

I go on a blind date in spring 2006, set up by a friend. The guy she wants me to meet seems really sweet over the phone and suggests we go to a lecture about Masaru Emoto, a Japanese author who believes that human consciousness has an effect on the molecular structure of water. I don't like going out to bars or dance clubs, or really anything that involves people pretending to be someone they aren't, so this sounds like a great first date to me.

When we arrive at the lecture, we learn that two people are speaking, a man and a woman. The energy of the man surprises me; he is touted as a spiritual guru, yet I see extreme ego in him. The woman fascinates me. Her energy is in the shadows, I can't see her clearly. I am looking at her directly, yet I can't grasp the structure of her face. She feels "clean" to me energetically, meaning she isn't emitting any negative energy and also isn't allowing other people's energy to come into her space. She is powerful, aware of her own boundaries, and capable of being a very strong vessel for Universal life force.

She introduces herself as a shaman.

I am not surprised. A voice very clearly in the center of my forehead tells me to introduce myself to her—God's guidance, once again. After the lecture, I excuse myself from my blind date, this sweet yet innocuous man, and walk up to the shaman. After I introduce myself, she says, "I know who you are, I've been waiting a long time to meet you."

This wildly unexpected comment startles me. I compose myself and say I believe I am supposed to train with her. Again, her unexpected response, "Yes, you are. We will begin next week."

Thus began a two-year intensive training with Susan, a Celtic shaman from Wales, who led our sacred gatherings from her suburban home in Delaware. In her candlelit basement, I joined five other women, all of us learning to traverse the veils between worlds through shamanic journeying—a practice of altered consciousness that opens doorways to spirit beings and animal guides.

My heart nearly stopped during my first journey to meet my animal totem. There, in the ethereal mists of the spirit world, stood a magnificent white tiger—its crystalline fur gleaming like fresh snow, eyes blazing with ancient wisdom. In that moment, time collapsed. I recognized this majestic being as the same protective presence that had watched over me throughout my childhood, the "imaginary" friend who stood guard during my darkest nights in the poster over my bed. But nothing was imaginary about this encounter. The white tiger's power and protection had been real all along.

The tiger's presence in my adult journeywork validated every childhood memory of feeling safely wrapped in its protective energy. Its massive form, both gentle and fierce, embodied the perfect balance of power and grace. When our eyes met during journeys, I felt the same profound connection that comforted me as a little girl—a bond that transcended time and space.

We learned to drum, our rhythms opening pathways to lower, upper, and middle worlds in search of healing wisdom. We embraced sacred ceremonies for personal and community healing, working with the four elements—fire, earth, water, and air—to deepen our connection with all that is. But it was always the white tiger who guided me most surely through these spiritual landscapes, its protective presence as steady and true as it was on the poster in my childhood bedroom.

In shamanism I find permission to exist as all of who I am, not as fragments of memories, and not in response to my family. Not as someone whose job it is to keep everyone else alive. Not as the master interpreter for all the alters. Not as a jumbled, confused mess of my emotions and the emotions of others. As a reconstructed self. An individuated being. My soul self.

Shamanic training helps me to make sense of darkness and light, the underbelly of the human condition that I had experienced as a child. In the world of the shaman, both darkness and light are present and necessary. One cannot exist without the other. There is no fear of death in shamanism. Death is not other, to be avoided or whitewashed with promises of heaven and eternal life. Death is simply a transformation and a necessary part of evolving as a soul.

At the end of my two-year training is a shamanic initiation—a "death of the ego" ceremony. This is the closing ritual that all six of us experience in order to graduate and become shamanic practitioners. Unlike a physical death, the shamanic death involves the dissolution of limiting beliefs, fears, and attachments to the ego. It's a process where the lower aspects of our selves—those tied to insecurity, comfort zones, or material attachments—are metaphorically "claimed" by spiritual forces.

My shamanic initiation wasn't just a ceremony—it was a death and rebirth. For the first time, I glimpsed who I truly was, beneath the layers of reactive survival patterns, beyond the girl who existed solely as a response to others' needs, trauma, and family chaos.

In the weeks leading up to the initiation, my back completely locked up, my body speaking what my mind couldn't yet accept. This physical rebellion was profound—it was as if my spine, the very foundation of my being, was refusing to carry the weight of everyone else's lives any longer. Each stabbing pain echoed an ancient truth: A body trained to respond only to trauma eventually forgets how to dance to its own rhythm.

Spiritually, this crippling back pain revealed a deeper message. It was the physical manifestation of decades of over-giving, of silencing my own voice, of burying my desires so deeply they became ghosts haunting my own house. I had become so adept at anticipating and managing others' needs that I had forgotten how to recognize my own reflection in the mirror.

The Universe wasn't subtle. My entire modus operandi—the hyper-vigilant caretaker, the teenage Atlas holding up a family's world—was being summoned to die. Yet I fought this death with every fiber of my being, clinging to the identity that had kept me alive through the darkest years. This version of myself, though wounded, was familiar. She was reliable. She knew how to survive. But survival, I was learning, was no longer enough.

On the day of my initiation, my shaman sisters gathered around me in our teacher's basement. I was laid out naked on a massage table, then covered in a blanket that had been blessed and used only for this sacred event. I was at the threshold between worlds. My two years of Celtic shamanic training had taught me that initiations aren't just about endings—they're portals to transformation. This was a sacred passage of spiritual metamorphosis.

My sisters beat their drums. The heartbeat rhythms echo the pulse of the life itself, creating the bridge between ordinary and nonordinary reality.

In Celtic tradition, ceremonies and initiations are moments of profound surrender. Like the turning of leaves in autumn, we release what no longer serves—old identities, worn beliefs, outdated ways of being. My own ceremony felt like standing in the heart of a storm while remaining perfectly still, watching parts of myself dissolve into mist.

What appeared as an ending became a catalyst for extraordinary rebirth. As the ceremony deepened, I experienced this ancient wisdom firsthand.

The initial dissolution felt like being unmade by starlight—each fixed point of my identity slowly releasing its hold. There was a moment when I existed in the space between breaths, between heartbeats, between what was and what would be. The drums carried me through this void, their rhythm a lifeline in the vast unknown.

Then came the rebuilding—not as a return to what was but as an emergence into something entirely new. Like the way crystals form in the earth's depths under tremendous pressure, this ceremonial death crafted new facets of being. Each breath drew in not just air but possibility. Each heartbeat synchronized with an ancient rhythm that had always been there, waiting to be remembered.

The Celts understand that true transformation requires complete surrender to this process of unbecoming. As the initiation drew to its close, I felt myself reassembling like mist condensing into morning dew, familiar yet fundamentally changed. The person who emerged carried the same name but resonated at a different frequency, saw through different eyes, moved through the world with a different understanding of its mysteries.

This wasn't just change—it was alchemical transformation, the kind our ancestors knew in their bones. The kind that turns the lead of old stories into the gold of new possibilities.

What happened to me on the other side of that shamanic initiation was remarkable. My spiritual reconstruction reverberated, and I was seen by my Quaker community in new ways. The Quaker spiritual community and center, where I had been living and working for a few years as a hospitality coordinator, invited me to begin leading their Young Adult Leadership Development Program, where I was charged with helping college-age students develop as spiritual leaders. My Quaker community also recognized me as a minister in 2007. Thus began another form of evolution in addition to my developing as a psychic and shaman.

Then my shamanism teacher told me I needed to go to seminary. I heard God's voice coming through her, guiding me even more deeply into the ministry.

In Quakerism, you don't have to go to seminary to become a minister. Quakers believe that people are called to the ministry, and the Quaker community, or elders, identify the gift of ministry in those who are called. But seminary is an option for deeper religious instruction.

Going to seminary was never part of my master plan, although people teased me that with the last name of *Churchman*, I should have known from childhood that my calling was to the ministry. But thanks to being raised as a Christian Scientist, and then as a Quaker, I believed that women could be ministers and hold positions of power in religion and in spiritual institutions.

I ended up going to seminary because I was trying to answer my question of what it meant for me to be a Quaker, a psychic, and also a shaman. Were these theologies competing, complementary, or just stepping stones for a new theological evolution? I was also still trying to figure out who I was, not in reaction to Debby or being who she needed me to be.

About six months before I began seminary, Bryce's three young children found him unconscious on their living room floor one Saturday morning. Twenty-two years after his first overdose at twelve, he once again overdosed, this time on heroin. He was hospitalized and in a coma for a week.

Bryce and his wife both managed sobriety for the first eight years of their relationship as they successfully parented their kids. But then something happened, and now they were both hooked on heroin again. Bryce's wife was handling it better than he was.

Debby went to the hospital to be with Bryce and to show up as a dutiful grandmother to her grandbabies. She found yet another detox program and got Bryce checked in. I had lost count of how many times he'd detoxed or how many times Debby had admitted him. I had to stop caring in order to save myself.

Every time Bryce used drugs was a sucker punch to my gut. Every time he went into a detox program I found myself catching my breath, wondering if this time it would finally stick, always to discover it didn't. He was a roller-coaster ride I could never get off of, even when we had no contact.

Could I have prevented his addiction when it began when he was twelve? Would it have been possible to save him from this life? How much longer can he remain alive this way? Would it be better if he just died?

I don't want to have these questions rolling around in my mind. I want the ride to fucking end. I know it's going to end with death. Every time I hear from my family, I expect the news that Bryce is dead. I resent him for choosing his addiction over the well-being of his family and children. I want him dead so I can get off this never-ending ride. Closure seems impossible without death.

I keep thinking it must be a choice. Tracy must have chosen to perpetuate the sexual abuse. Debby must have chosen to create alternative personalities. Dad must have chosen to become physically abusive. Bryce must have chosen to use drugs. What is wrong with these people that keeps them from making different choices?

I didn't understand addiction, or multiplicity, or the cycle of abuse in families. My brain couldn't compute it. We came from the same family.

How is it that I am able to make such different choices from my other family members?

"But you're so strong," my friends tell me. "You're resilient. That's why your life differs from Bryce's and your family's." I don't feel resilient or strong. The only difference I can discern is that my foundational orientation is toward staying alive and living life. I think I came out of Debby's womb this way. I am an old soul choosing to play full out in this game called life.

Debby became Bryce's medical power of attorney. She stepped up and became responsible for him in all the ways she couldn't when we were little. I was grateful that he had her support. I was jealous that she was giving her attention to the one of us who looked like he was hurting the most.

I'm much better at hiding my pain. I am the forgotten one, even in adulthood, because I appear to be a functional adult.

Shortly after this, Bryce's wife and children moved to another state to be closer to her grandparents, who had raised her. Bryce never recovered from losing them. He returned to what he knew—living on the streets and continuing his long-standing relationship with drugs.

CHAPTER TWENTY-FIVE
SEMINARY

I began seminary in January 2010. I was thirty-five, and ready for my next stage of growth, not just becoming another version of myself like Debby and the alters but becoming a more complete version of who I have always been at soul level. I was actively reconstructing myself.

Seminary helped me to integrate as a Quaker, a psychic, and a shaman. Seminary also opened me to scripture in unexpected ways, inviting me to wrestle with my own theology and providing a strong foundation for me to continue to teach undergraduates about spiritual formation. In my first week of classes, I realized a deep longing to continue to work with young adults on spiritual issues, just as I had at the Quaker Center in Philadelphia. Looking online, I saw that the college the seminary is affiliated with was advertising for a newly created position doing just that with Quaker students, with a same-day job application deadline.

Three weeks later I started this job, and I continued it throughout my time at seminary. Serving as administrative faculty for the college during seminary was life-giving because it allowed me to apply my seminary learning at work. I especially enjoyed teaching the under-graduates because of their continual life discernment and their willingness to look at their own constructed theology and consider what they wanted their relationships with God to be like.

The classroom became a sacred space of mutual discovery. Each time a student questioned their inherited beliefs or wrestled with divine purpose, I saw reflections of my own spiritual wrestling match.

Their fresh-faced determination to understand their place in the grand theological narrative reminded me of my own journey.

I'm on a similar journey as my students. Helping them in their discernment helps me in mine. This becomes an ongoing theme for me. Whatever I need to work on in myself, I help others work on in themselves.

In those moments of teaching and mentoring, I discovered a profound truth about healing: It rarely travels in a straight line. Like my students questioning their childhood beliefs, I too was dismantling and rebuilding my understanding of faith, family, and forgiveness. Each class discussion about divine love forced me to confront my own complicated relationship with unconditional acceptance. Every conversation about spiritual trauma opened new doors in my own healing journey.

The classroom was a laboratory for understanding how personal transformation and professional calling could intertwine, creating something more powerful than either could be alone. This parallel process—healing while helping others heal—would become the cornerstone of my professional life. It's a pattern that repeated itself through my work in the world.

In the first month of seminary, I began to have memories of Tracy sexually abusing me. I got fleeting glimpses of it—me, less than two years old, her, hovering above me.

It took a year for me to summon the courage to tell Debby 2 what I remembered.

"Mom, I need to tell you something really difficult."

Debby 2: "Um, okay."

Me: "I'm having memories of your mother sexually abusing me."

Debby 2: "That is not possible."

Me: "No, I'm telling you that I have very specific memories involving Tracy hurting me."

Debby 2: "There's no way she could have done that. I would have known if something was wrong."

Me: "Tracy sexually abused you too. That's what caused you to have so many alters."

Debby 2: "I don't know what you're talking about. There are no alters."

After that, I stopped speaking to Debby 2 because I accepted that she is only ever able to protect herself, even if it means causing harm to those closest to her.

The memories of the abuse, coupled with Debby 2's denial, caused me to no longer feel obligated to protect Debby's identity with my silence, as I had done for my entire life.

As a family, we hid the realities of our home life well from our social and faith communities. As the eldest child, my primary job was to be the great pretender, to help perpetuate the myth that we were "normal" and everything was "fine."

But we weren't normal. Nor were we fine. As a child I was terrified of my parents because I knew they were capable of killing me in their fits of rage and anger. I knew their depression and mental illness could easily cloud their love for me as they were pounding down doors I was hiding behind. I spent my childhood waiting for my parents to end their lives so I could feel safe.

In my own reconstruction I perceived that Debby was my captor. I was in bondage to her for over a quarter century. Her narcissism, cleverly hidden in endless personalities, disallowed my brothers and me from developing on our own. She successfully shaped us into beings who existed only for her or in reaction to her. Just as Debby always wanted—four children to love and adore her.

Debby also didn't understand my psychic work, or training as a shaman, or even going to seminary. I was evolving in ways that didn't make sense to her. We were becoming further and further apart from each other. The ache in my heart for a mother to care for me remained. But it had always been there. That was not new.

At this point, I decided to end my relationship with Debby. I could not continue my journey of unpacking my own trauma and healing from it with someone so close to me denying I was traumatized. This also meant pulling back from interacting with my brothers because they all wanted to be in a relationship with Debby. I didn't want to make them choose between her and me. Instead, I deselected myself from our family.

I railed against myself for making this decision, but I knew it was in the best interest of the boys and Debby for me to do so. I hated losing relationships with my brothers, especially Alex and Edward, who were my children too. I could feel they didn't understand what I was doing and took it personally when I stopped attending family gatherings and holidays or even calling to check on them. There was no way to explain what I was doing without causing them pain. But the only way I could continue to love them was by loving myself first.

This realization didn't come easily. For years, I operated from the belief that loving others meant sacrificing myself—that my worth was measured by how much I could give, how much I could endure, how seamlessly I could disappear into the needs of others. The Christian Science teachings of my childhood had reinforced this pattern, suggesting that my pain wasn't real, that my needs were somehow less valid than everyone else's. I learned to make myself small, to silence my voice, to numb my body's signals in the service of keeping peace.

But trauma recovery taught me a fundamental truth: You cannot pour from an empty cup. The very act of loving others requires that you first understand your own worth, your own boundaries, your own right to exist fully in this world. Self-love isn't selfish—it's the foundation upon which all healthy relationships are built.

Setting boundaries with my family initially felt like betrayal. Every missed holiday, every unanswered call, every moment I chose my healing over their comfort triggered waves of guilt that threatened to pull me back into old patterns. The voice in my head screamed that I was abandoning them, that I was being cruel, that a good person would find a way to maintain these relationships without putting herself in danger.

But I was learning to distinguish between guilt and intuition, between the voice of trauma and the voice of wisdom. My body—the same body I had been taught to distrust and silence—was finally speaking truth. The anxiety that spiked before family gatherings, the exhaustion that followed every interaction, the way I lost pieces of myself in their presence—these were not signs of weakness but signals of a nervous system trying to protect me.

Self-love meant honoring these signals. It meant recognizing that my emotional and spiritual well-being mattered as much as anyone else's. It meant understanding that I could not be truly present for others while I was fragmenting inside, that the love I offered from a place of depletion was not the love anyone deserved.

The hardest part was accepting that loving myself might look like cruelty to others. Alex and Edward, still children in many ways, could only see my absence as rejection. They couldn't understand that my withdrawal was not about them but about creating space for my own healing—space that had never existed in our family system. They couldn't see that by learning to love myself, I was modeling something revolutionary: that it was possible to exist without constantly sacrificing my essence for others' comfort.

For years, erasing myself from my family felt like a knife stabbing me in my heart. I stopped seeing any of them in person and rarely spoke with them by phone. I spent many holidays alone, not allowing myself permission to *enjoy* living without my family. I felt immense guilt for having left my brothers. Why couldn't I reconstruct myself *with* them?

I grieved my favorite part of the holiday season: singing Christmas carols with Debby. Sitting in the living room, next to each other on the couch draped in blue, we went through the entire large-print songbook. We knew 95 percent of the songs and sang them all. The ones we didn't like that much we'd just sing the first verse or two. We harmonized our voices. Debby was always a good singer, and the majority of my positive early childhood memories are of her singing to me or with me. When I was very little, she played her guitar while she sang, and Bryce and I danced around the room to the music.

Debby recommended books she thought I would like. She always had exceptional taste in books and took me to the library from a very early age, encouraging my love of reading. I relied on her to find books, and I always loved the ones she chose.

All of that stopped when I stepped away from my family.

Self-love meant grieving the fantasy of the family I had always wanted—the one where I could be both daughter and mother, where I could heal while maintaining all the relationships that had shaped me. It meant accepting that some relationships cannot survive the transition from dysfunction to health, that choosing wholeness sometimes meant choosing solitude.

But in that solitude, I discovered something significant: When I truly love myself, when I honor my own needs and boundaries, the love I have to offer others becomes pure. It's no longer tangled with resentment, codependency, or the desperate need for validation. It becomes a choice rather than a compulsion, a gift rather than a transaction.

Self-love opened my heart to recognize and nurture the relationships that could actually sustain me. I reached out to my aunt and uncle—Debby's older sister and her husband—and asked them to spiritually adopt me. This wasn't a casual request born from loneliness; it was a deliberate choice to seek the parental love and guidance I had never received. My aunt and uncle had remained childless by choice, and I sensed in them a capacity for the kind of steady, unconditional love that had been absent from my childhood.

Our relationship had been building for years. Since college, I had gravitated toward their home during holidays and summer breaks, drawn to the peace that existed within their walls. There was no walking on eggshells, no scanning the room for signs of which personality might emerge, no bracing for emotional storms. In their presence, I could simply be—a radical experience for someone who had spent her formative years managing everyone else's emotional weather.

When I asked them to become my chosen parents, they embraced the role with the same quiet grace they brought to everything else. They became voices of wisdom and gentle guidance, consistently affirming that caring for myself wasn't selfish—it was essential. They witnessed my healing journey without trying to fix me, offering the kind of stable presence I had always craved.

Their response to my estrangement from my birth family revealed the depth of their understanding. Without my asking, my aunt and uncle too stepped back from contact with Debby and my brothers. This wasn't about choosing sides; it was about recognizing that the chaos and dysfunction that had shaped my childhood were still actively harmful to anyone who remained entangled in it. Their decision to prioritize their own well-being while supporting mine showed me what healthy boundaries looked like in practice.

In choosing them, and in their choosing me back, I learned that family isn't just about blood—it's about who shows up consistently, who celebrates your growth, and who loves you not despite your healing but because of your courage to pursue it.

Self-love is not a destination but a daily practice. It's choosing to speak kindly to yourself when the world feels harsh. It's hand-picking relationships that are life-giving. It's honoring your body's needs even when others call you selfish. It's setting boundaries even when they disappoint people you care about. It's believing that your healing matters, that your peace matters, that your very existence has value beyond what you can provide for others.

This is the foundation of all trauma recovery: the radical act of believing you are worthy of love, especially your own.

CHAPTER TWENTY-SIX
MINISTRY

Apparently my prayer a decade earlier of "Where the fuck are you, God?" worked because by the time I got to seminary, God and I were together all the time.

A year into seminary, God told me to start a spiritual direction practice. Walking home from classes one day, a clear voice in the middle of my forehead said, "It's time for you to open your own healing practice."

I did some of this work for the six years I lived in Philadelphia, but never on a full-time basis. I had Reiki and Energy Healing clients, as well as clients like my friend Amy who wanted me to help clear their houses of spirits.

I squelched that side gig, though, after I got a call to clear a very old house outside of Philadelphia that had been featured on the TV show *Ghost Hunters*. The house was previously a jail, a courthouse, and a brothel. It was full of spirits at various stages of unrest. The *Ghost Hunters* filming stirred up all the spirits, and by the time I got there, chaos had ensued. It was too much for me to handle, and I realized that I wanted to attend to the living more than the dead. Helping college students figure out their own theology and spiritual leadership was more life-giving for me.

So I said to God, "Fine, if you want me to have a private practice I'll do it, but you have to bring me clients because I don't have time to do marketing or outreach." Within two months I was seeing ten clients a week, using the marketing strategy of answering my phone.

I know God has a sense of humor with me. Honestly, I'm not sure how most of these people found me. I didn't have a website, and my business wasn't listed in the yellow pages.

My own spirituality deepened significantly as I accompanied others on their spiritual journeys. I began to step into my own role as a spiritual leader. My clients were seminary students and pastors, healers, faculty members, farmers, factory workers, hairdressers, nurses, and doctors. They asked timeless theological questions such as, "Why did God do this to me?" "What is God asking of me in this situation?" "How do I find God in this person I can't stand?" I didn't have the answers to all of these questions, but I found myself increasingly more comfortable with joining my clients in wrestling with them.

While sitting across from my clients, I began to sort through the chaos of my own emotions. I observed them struggling and could see so clearly when their egos were protecting them versus when their emotions were honoring the truth of who they were. In this witnessing, I was also learning more about how to honor my own truth, a process I began in seminary.

Spirituality allowed me to consciously reconstruct myself instead of just reacting to my family. My upset about my brothers' addictions to drugs and alcohol became acknowledging that we each have free will. We each are fully capable, in each moment, of making different choices, despite our background and experiences.

My frustration with Debby splitting into so many personalities turned into recognizing what a phenomenal coping mechanism it was for extreme abuse. She found a way, in her mind, to cope by fragmenting herself off from those horrific experiences.

My rage against Dad became remembering the parts of him that I loved, recognizing his impact on my love of music and art and his cultivation of my intelligence.

Every time I helped someone heal their own trauma and strengthen their own relationship with God, I experienced healing. I experienced comfort. I experienced moving beyond just surviving trauma. I experienced being in right relationship with my emotions. Addressing their trauma required that I heal mine. I had to stop seeing myself as a victim of abuse, neglect, or bad parenting. Once I began perceiving myself as a soul who chose this life for myself, I began to see that everything that had ever happened had happened *for* me.

Trauma caused Debby to split and caused me to reconstruct myself in a different way by becoming the most complete version of me. From her I learned that reconstruction was an option for myself, having witnessed it countless times in my childhood. But what's the difference between reconstructing yourself in order to survive and reconstructing yourself in order to thrive? I was trying to thrive, but I had no role models for that.

I was muddling my way through, with whispers of guidance from God in the center of my forehead.

Two years into seminary, I was yearning for more hands-on practice with what I was learning. Identifying texts in the Bible seemed less important than accompanying people through a dark night of the soul or through experiences that confronted or expanded their theology and relationship with God.

Because it was a requirement to graduate from seminary, I applied for a clinical pastoral education (CPE) residency in a hospital setting. I was admitted to a CPE program in a 150-bed hospital outside of Asheville, North Carolina, that catered to a Southern Baptist population.

Don, my first CPE supervisor, was a Southern Baptist who participated in Native rituals with the local Cherokee population. He was also a recovering alcoholic and twelve-stepper. My heart leapt in kinship the moment we met. My fear of not being Christian enough, ministerial enough, able to pray out loud enough, compassionate enough, Biblically literate enough, or mainstream enough instantly dissipated. Don immediately got me at a soul level.

Don showed me that I didn't have to fit into a particular box in order to be a "real" hospital chaplain. He was excited to have a Quaker minister and shamanic practitioner trained at his hospital. My being psychic didn't seem to faze him in the slightest. Don taught me that I was born to be a chaplain and that we are all on a spiritual journey, whether we call it that or not. I felt integrated as a Quaker minister/ shaman/psychic in his presence.

The memories of being sexually abused by Tracy continued during this time. I had several experiences in the hospital of attending to patients and getting triggered by hearing their stories of sexual abuse.

A rape victim came into the ER and didn't want to report her abuser. In fact, she wanted to go home with him. I got so angry with her (in my mind) for her wanting to return to the abuse.

Why doesn't she think that she deserves better? What is wrong with her for not being stronger?

Really, I was railing against Debby, against all of the things I wished she had figured out before she had children.

A comatose baby was admitted to the pediatric ICU. The diagnosis was shaken baby syndrome, a serious brain injury caused by someone forcefully shaking an infant. The mother was more concerned about the father's being a diabetic and not having anything to eat than her own child's well-being. I found myself wanting to interrogate both parents to determine the culprit and then annihilate that parent. When Child Protective Services got involved, I had to take a step back and let the professionals do their jobs. I transferred my parents onto those parents, thinking if I could fix them, maybe I could make more sense of my own upbringing.

It was hard to know exactly what was going on and not be able to fix the problems. I wanted to protect these people in the ways I had never been protected.

I had learned to be the fixer and protector in my family for everyone else. I became so good at it that no one ever guessed we had problems. It became my way of coping with the trauma. Now I wanted to apply my highly refined skill set to every patient.

The chaplaincy residents took turns working in different hospital departments. A fellow resident took over my rotation in the emergency department. He started handling cases much differently than I would—trying to bring family members back to see patients when they were still being assessed and providing family members with more information than I did. I took the approach of gathering information first, in case any family members were involved in the patient's injury. He thought being together as a family was most important.

The other resident came from a family dynamic where being together was safe and a good thing. I came from a dynamic where family was dangerous and not to be trusted. I told him during a residents' meeting that he wasn't qualified to assess and attend to patients and their families because he wasn't being cautious enough. In the heat of the moment, I blurted out, "You don't know what you're doing, and you need to stay out of my ER."

My childhood tendency to defy authority and think I knew better than everyone else reared its ugly head during this residency. Somehow, my big mouth always opened up outside of our family. As long as I wasn't related to them, I had no problem telling other people when I thought they were doing something wrong.

I apologized later for being a know-it-all. I had to set aside my sense of rightness about how trauma should be attended to and recognize that my actions toward patients and family members often came from my own trauma response instead of what was actually happening.

I had to learn to self-soothe in those moments, to recover my own trauma in the present moment as I was attending to patients. I reminded myself that I was safe. I processed my experiences by writing them out. I consciously tried to be kind to myself instead of beating myself up for having feelings. Through trial and error, I learned that these situations were not about me. Most importantly, I learned to stop trying to fix everyone else and instead to meet them in their brokenness—something I was always terrified of doing in my own family.

CHAPTER TWENTY-SEVEN
MIDWIFE FOR THE HOLY

Psychotraumatologist Dr. Peter Levine says that trauma can be a gateway to profound spiritual transformation and awakening. I believe that it was for me. Spirituality was my pathway for healing my childhood trauma and my portal for reconstructing my soul self, the essence of who I have always been.

I did a second year of clinical pastoral education residency at a bustling Level 1 trauma center in Tennessee, the only center offering the highest level of trauma care in a 150-mile radius. There, I discovered that I was a trauma junkie. In my earlier residency, the world made sense to me the first time I was paged to the emergency department for a dying patient. I was hooked. Working as a trauma chaplain in my second residency, I came to understand that many people who work in trauma (doctors and nurses, emergency service personnel, police, firefighters, sheriffs, etc.) are drawn to it because they have experienced trauma themselves.

From my own family, I viscerally understood what it's like to experience physical, sexual, emotional, and spiritual abuse. In chaplaincy, I was given an opportunity to use the coping skills I had developed in response to that trauma and get paid a salary, as opposed to shelling out money for therapy to overcome my ingrained coping skills. The deep shame I carried from my trauma began transforming itself into hope. Being able to set aside my own trauma and be fully present for someone else's was a healing form of self-preservation for me.

Within the CPE program container, with the support of my supervisor, Larry, I learned how to transform the horror I experienced as a child into something beautiful and life-giving for others, without compromising my own well-being. I learned how to be fully present in other people's traumatic situations, without retraumatizing myself and without ignoring parts of myself like I had as a teenager, and like Debby learned to do so well.

It was oddly comforting and familiar to be with others during their trauma experiences. I was at peace when standing in a trauma bay with a screaming patient lying on the table, surrounded by doctors and nurses shouting orders, or with family members in the waiting room wailing for God. I knew how to breathe into that reality. I was calm and cool in the midst of the storm.

As a chaplain, my idea of a good day at work involved spending eight to twenty-four hours hanging out in the hospital's emergency department and intensive care units, attending to patients and their family members who had suffered significant emotional, spiritual, and physical trauma from altercations with other people, weapons, cars, trees, or natural disasters.

One day, in particular, stands out in my memory. Within a three-hour afternoon period, six people from five different incidents presented to the emergency department. There were two drivers who had hit each other in a motor vehicle collision, a man struck in the head and spine by a tree in a logging incident, a young man with a brain injury from a self-inflicted gunshot wound, a female patient in cardiac arrest, and a deceased four-year-old boy whose death went unpronounced by EMS at the scene—even trained professionals couldn't bear to speak those final words over a child's dead body. The level of anxiety and fear in the emergency department was palpable. The patients and their family members were terrified. The trauma team pivoted between trauma bays, their expertise stretched thin as they triaged multiple critical cases competing for the same urgent resources.

That afternoon wasn't the first time that I had wrapped my arms around an inconsolable mother, rocking her gently in the small, uncomfortable room at the edges of the emergency department's waiting area. But it was the first time I held a mother without desiring to console her—to take away her pain and release her from what I knew would become an unending grief. It was the first time I blamed a mother for her young son's death.

I first knew only bits and pieces about what had brought this mother and her four-year-old son into the ER that day. The emergency medical services medics mentioned that police had been called to the scene. The trauma pager message I had responded to indicated that the child was found unresponsive and unconscious in his front yard. I overheard the mother talking by phone with her thirteen-year-old nephew, who was found alone with her son. He told her that her son had fallen off a bed and hit his head. She didn't ask why the police had found her son outside instead of inside, which contradicted what her nephew told her.

I found it odd that the mother asked so few questions about her young son. Also odd was that it was virtually impossible to keep her within the hospital walls. She kept running out into the parking lot, as if not being in the hospital would prevent her son from being dead.

After the boy was officially pronounced deceased, the pediatric doctors and I went to the parking lot to tell his mother. Her first response was to ask if the ER team was still treating her son. "No," the doctors said. "Your son is dead." "Is he still breathing?" she asked. The doctors looked at her, confused. Then she ran to the far end of the hospital parking lot. One of the hospital security guards had to restrain her from running into the street.

She refused to hear about how her child died. She had to be cajoled back through the hospital doors to see her son's body, and when she finally did, she only stayed for three minutes. She didn't ask any questions about how he died and seemed to believe her nephew's story that her son hit his head when he fell off a bed. She mentioned that she had a seven-month-old daughter but seemed completely unconcerned about her whereabouts. When her ten-year-old daughter arrived at the hospital, she looked at her for a moment, then promptly ignored her.

Her son's death seemed to be all about her and how she didn't want to live in the world anymore. When her sister arrived (the mother of the thirteen-year-old nephew), she ignored her as well, until the sister said she had to go to the police station to get her son. Then both the mother and I knew that the nephew had been taken into custody.

Parents respond to death in different ways. I just intuitively felt like there was something more going on with this mother not wanting to know how her son died. I also found it strange that when she went into the ER room to see her son's body, the first thing she did was uncover him to look at his private parts. It seemed like she knew her son was being sexually abused.

It wasn't until later that afternoon, when the sheriff walked into the ER and asked me where the gunshot victim was, that I started to get actual information about what had happened. It took me a hot minute to realize that the sheriff was asking about the four-year-old boy. I had been so caught up in attending to the mother that I hadn't gotten any details about what actually had caused the boy's death.

The ER team initially surmised that a BB gun pellet to the heart killed the boy, but a CT scan showed that it was an actual bullet. Because of the confusion over what the nephew told the mother about how the boy was hurt, one of the nurses trained in forensics suggested doing a CT scan of the entire body.

The scan revealed that the boy's liver was full of blood from a severe laceration. A trauma surgeon explained to me that this would have occurred as a result of the child's stomach or back being stomped on by someone much larger than him on the same day he was shot. The CT also revealed that the boy's rectum had been violated as well. I didn't learn this until the next morning, when the ER manager brought me up to speed with the case.

I wept in the manager's office. That mother who hadn't protected her four-year-old son reminded me too much of Debby, oblivious to everything happening to her children outside of how it affected her emotionally. Waiting for other people to pick up the pieces so she could focus on being in her own emotional chaos. Knowing what was really going on but pretending she didn't.

I held my anger toward that mother in the ER, but it came out once I was safely in the confines of the ER manager's office. The manager knew what was really going on too. So did everyone on the trauma team, both pediatric and adult. We all knew; we all witnessed what had happened to that poor boy. But there was nothing we could do. The case was in the hands of the police, and, hopefully, Child Protective Services.

I prayed for the siblings of the boy who died—the seven-month-old and ten-year-old daughters. May they be held and comforted. May they be safe. May they never know the horror of being physically violated.

May they be taken away from their mother.

I thought about what would have happened if my brothers and I had been taken away from Debby. How would our lives have unfolded? For me, I may never have been called to the ministry, or gone to seminary, or found myself in an ER attending to a pediatric abuse case. Maybe my psychic skills wouldn't have developed. Maybe I wouldn't have had the courage, or the capacity, to launch my first business when I was only twenty-four. Maybe I wouldn't know how to help others attend to their own trauma as I healed mine.

I thought of the Christian Science volunteer chaplain who also had the opportunity to attend to this family but instead prayed for them, from a distance, in the on-call room. Her response epitomized my entire issue with that religion—denial of the fittest. If you pretend it isn't happening to you, then you won't be sick. If you keep yourself at arm's length from the destruction and the devastation, then it won't be real. Or at least that's what I learned by osmosis as a child.

I thought about what drew Debby to Christian Science in the first place. Was it because she liked being punished if she got sick, when she was told that it was because she wasn't praying enough? Or maybe she liked that she never had to take her children to doctors, so no one would ever know they were being abused. If she had, maybe they would have discovered that Tracy had raped both Bryce and me. Maybe they would have seen the bruises from Dad hitting Bryce or the track marks on Bryce's arms from his drug usage at such a young age.

By the time I left the mother and the ER that afternoon, I still had fifteen hours left of my twenty-four-hour shift. On days like this, I tried to pace myself, because I literally had no idea what would happen during my long shift. I prayed into those days, asking God to guide my ministry when I was too spent to think clearly.

When the pager went off yet again that day, after my third attempt to lie down to sleep in my on-call room, I prayed that God would show me how to be present to the patient and family I was about to encounter in the middle of the night. I also prayed that God would wake me up enough to find the back door to the ER at 3:00 a.m. Then I prayed that God would ease my heart enough for me to fall back asleep again.

Sometimes, I left the hospital feeling faith-filled and well-used. Other days, I just went straight to bed and didn't get up until I had to go to work again.

As a hospital chaplain, I also met many people who had attempted suicide. I learned surprising things—that shooting yourself in the head in order to enact death isn't actually as easy as it looks in the movies and that a botched suicide attempt can rid you of your personality and capacity to even feed or bathe yourself. Each encounter with a patient or family of a suicide helped me to begin reconciling my own experience of suicide and suicidal ideation with my family members.

I spoke with many patients who shot themselves in the head or overdosed on pills and lived to talk about it. Each one expressed gratitude very clearly for still being alive once they were able to see the outpouring of love from family members, friends, and their faith communities. These patients told me they didn't know they were loved and wanted in this world until after they attempted suicide.

My heart wept for them in their unknowing. Attending to them lessened my anger toward Debby and Dad. Witnessing the broken-ness in suicidal patients and their family members offered me a sense of grace about my own family's compulsion toward suicide.

As a hospital chaplain, I held family members wailing on the ground, praying to God for a miracle when a doctor told them that their loved one was dead or would eventually die when the bleeding in the brain caused by a gunshot wound swelled enough to cause significant brain injury. There was no comfort or end to the grief for these families.

I was with mothers, fathers, wives, husbands, sons, and daughters screaming in the ER at their dead family member, telling them that they should have known they were loved and there were other ways to end the pain. "Do you want to die, or do you want to end the pain?" became the first thing I asked when I was referred to a patient who had attempted suicide or who wanted to. Most of the time they just wanted the pain to stop but could not conceive of any way to end their pain other than death.

Helping others heal from trauma was a path of healing from my own. This is what calmed my internal anger toward my family and my grief of what I missed out on in my childhood.

Challenge makes us bitter or better. I chose the empowered path, becoming the person who could not only attend to my own suffering but also the suffering of others. In those sacred spaces between life and death, joy and sorrow, I became the steady presence that staff, patients, and families turned to when they felt alone, afraid, over-whelmed, happy, excited, exhausted, or worn out. I was the witness and the accompanier, standing in the gap between human suffering and divine presence.

The years I spent navigating Debby's personalities had unknow-ingly prepared me for this holy work. Each encounter with trauma in the hospital corridors echoed with the familiar rhythms of my own story, yet now I stood on the other side—not as the wounded child but as the wounded healer.

I was a midwife for the Holy—not just delivering comfort but helping birth new understanding in the midst of chaos. I held hands, prayed, found warm blankets, and brought hot coffee to those who needed it. I cried; I laughed; I remained silent when there were no words that could bring comfort. I laid my hands on those who were suffering and wept with them, my own childhood wounds becoming a bridge of understanding.

Sometimes I prayed verbally, but often silently, letting the holy silence speak what words could not. I wiped away tears, and I hugged equally into grief and joy, my body becoming a vessel for divine comfort. I placed my hands on the heads of doctors, nurses, emergency workers, helicopter pilots, and police officers, and blessed them—these warriors of healing who carried their own invisible wounds. I asked God to protect them and keep them safe, to keep their hearts open to those they served, even as I recognized how my own heart had remained open despite everything with Debby.

From unpacking my own theology in seminary, I believe that God created us, but that God also gives humans the choice to live into God's will for us. This understanding was hard-won through the crucible of my childhood. I don't believe that God causes suffering; I do believe that God suffers alongside us, just as God suffered with me through those tumultuous years with Debby.

God is the Great Physician and Teacher, the Source of all that is and all that shall be, the Eternal Spirit, Creator, the Pain Bearer, the Great Mystery, the Holy, and the Mother and Father of us all. God is with us in our most trying moments and in our deepest sorrow. God was present in every fractured personality I encountered in my mother and in every broken soul I met in the trauma center. God celebrates with us and wraps us in loving arms while we weep. God hears our prayers, even the ones too deep for words.

God offers healing, but not always in the ways we imagine healing to be possible. Sometimes healing comes through helping others heal. For me, serving as a chaplain in the two hospitals, first in the rural 150-bed facility and then in the Level 1 trauma center, offered significant healing and helped me to process my own trauma, loss, and emotions so I could stop living in reaction to them. It also showed me that I no longer wanted to live in chaos, including working at a busy hospital as a trauma chaplain. This realization eventually led me to create a different kind of healing space, one where I could teach others to transform their trauma into triumph, just as I had done.

CHAPTER TWENTY-EIGHT
THE ENTREPRENEUR

For decades, chaos felt safer to me than calm. Like a familiar blanket woven from crisis and urgency, it wrapped around my nervous system, convincing me that living on high alert was not just acceptable but necessary. The constant state of emergency in my childhood home had trained me to believe that living to help others was more noble than helping myself. Trauma wasn't just something I experienced—it had become my reason for existing, my North Star in a stormy sea.

But now I had chosen to no longer live with chaos, and this decision revealed my hardest life lesson yet. *If there is no trauma to fix, no crisis to manage, then who am I?* The question echoed in the unfamiliar silence of my calmer life, challenging everything I thought I knew about myself. Without the constant drumbeat of others' needs, I had to confront the terrifying task of discovering my own rhythm.

The changes I made were decisive and absolute. I stepped away from my role as a hospital trauma chaplain, where every day had fed my addiction to crisis. I completely severed communication with my family, a surgical cut to stop the bleeding of generational trauma. I blocked Debby on my phone, letting her attempts at communication fall into the void of my new boundaries. Each action felt like amputating a part of myself that, though diseased, had been with me since birth.

The initial silence was deafening. Without the familiar symphony of trauma and chaos, without the daily drama from my family, I felt untethered. Putting myself first—a radical act of self-preservation— left me feeling isolated and unanchored. Sadness became my constant companion, not because I missed the chaos but because I was mourning the person I had been, the role I had played for so long.

In need of both income and transition, I found middle ground as a part-time home hospice chaplain in rural Western North Carolina. This gentler version of chaplaincy became my bridge between worlds. There, death wasn't a sudden, violent visitor but an expected guest. My patients and their families had already made peace with what was coming. Gone was the frenetic energy of the ER. In its place were quiet bedside conversations, gentle moments of connection, and the sacred space of accepted endings. That year of sitting with the dying taught me how to live differently. It helped me recalibrate my internal compass away from the magnetic pull of chaos and trauma, showing me that I could still be of service without sacrificing myself in the process.

In 2014, when I was forty years old, I became a full-time spiritual advisor to entrepreneurs and business leaders, helping them navigate their own journeys of transformation while secretly teaching myself the same lessons. This wasn't just a career change—it was my sacred laboratory for manifesting desires. Having spent years as a minister and chaplain, processing others' pain in real time, I was ready to transform my own experiences into something more expansive. Stepping into the transformative realm of full-time business owner-ship and entrepreneurship became my path of evolution.

When I was a child, desire was dangerous. The simple act of choosing toilet paper at the grocery store paralyzed me; years of adapting to others' needs had so completely muted my own inner compass that even the smallest preferences felt foreign.

Desire, I learned, is the language of the soul. Each tentative step toward naming what I wanted—first in business, then in life—became a ritual of reclamation. Creating a new business became my bridge between who I was and who I was becoming. This separate entity—my company—served as a safe container for practicing manifestation, for daring to want more, for learning to trust my intuition.

This new business venture became not an escape but a deliberate step toward expansion. While Debby created new personalities to hide from her truth, I launched this new enterprise to discover what I was truly capable of. It was a conscious choice to expand, not to fragment.

I became a method actor in my own life story, embodying the version of me that had already achieved what I desired, even if these things hadn't happened yet. While Debby retreated into her alters to escape the present, I reached forward into potential futures, inhabiting them as if they were already real.

I kept focusing on becoming the version of me that had already achieved the result, despite my current circumstances. Each new chapter of my business life wasn't an alternate personality taking over but rather my core self stepping more fully into its power. Running my own business aligned with my soul's calling. It was a radical act of self-trust, though it came with its own initiations and challenges.

That we can choose how to handle our wounds later became foundational to my trauma recovery work. We can either fragment like Debby, letting our pain shatter us into pieces, or we can integrate like I learned to do, using each challenge as a catalyst for conscious evolution.

Every step of claiming my desires led me here, to this moment of helping others claim theirs. Looking back, I see how this chapter in my life prepared me for standing before thousands of leaders, sharing tools for resilience and trauma recovery, teaching others how to transform their wounds into wisdom.

Being an entrepreneur forced me to confront my complicated relationship with authority. Growing up, I watched both my parents—Debby with her train car of personalities and my alcoholic father with his rages and his bouts of depression—fail repeatedly at their basic responsibilities. The authority figures who should have noticed our family's dysfunction remained silent, teaching me early that those in power couldn't be trusted. This lesson etched itself deep into my psyche, becoming both a wound and a source of strength.

This distrust made me a terrible employee. In my earlier adulthood, if I identified a better way to accomplish something, I wouldn't hesitate to march straight to my boss or the organization's leadership to point it out. Bureaucratic processes felt like another form of the gaslighting I'd experienced in childhood. I had no patience for systems designed to maintain the status quo rather than create real change or for keeping my head down or playing politics. My refusal to stay quiet about inefficiencies or poor leadership earned me a reputation as a troublemaker with multiple employers. But what they saw as insubordination was really my trauma-trained alertness rebelling at letting broken systems persist.

The transition to full-time entrepreneurship revealed a different kind of authority challenge. Soon after launching my coaching business, I manifested a $20,000 sales month. It happened quickly once I realized I could create any result I desired, just as I'd learned to create safety in impossible situations as a child. But this success triggered an unexpected crisis. I felt myself pressing against an invisible ceiling, a financial set point that threatened to pull me backward. I wanted to push forward, to expand, but prosperity felt as dangerous as chaos once had.

All the guilt about money my parents had programmed into me came flooding in like a toxic tide. In the heyday of their careers, they never earned more than a combined $50,000 a year, which did not stretch far in the Washington, DC metropolitan area. Growing up, scarcity was our constant companion. Money wasn't just tight, it was a source of anxiety that permeated our daily lives. We navigated the grocery store like treasure hunters, Debby clutching her carefully clipped coupons while I kept track of the running total in my head, terrified we'd reach the checkout counter and not have enough. Our clothes came from thrift store racks, where I learned to spot quality amid the castoffs, turning necessity into a skill that would later serve me well in business.

The highlight of our month was "Fun Friday"—Debby's attempt at creating normalcy in our chaotic world. She would give each of us five dollars to spend at the grocery store for dinner. It was meant to be liberating, but even then I felt the weight of responsibility. While my brothers would gleefully grab candy bars and sodas, I often chose practical items that could stretch into multiple meals, already shouldering the role of family caretaker.

But the real inheritance wasn't just financial scarcity—it was a toxic mythology about money itself. I was indoctrinated into believing that money wasn't safe, that it was a weapon wielded by the powerful (specifically Republicans) to control the vulnerable. The narrative in our home painted a stark picture: People with money were inherently greedy, and those who dared to spend it on themselves were selfish and morally bankrupt. This wasn't just about finances, it was a worldview that equated self-care with self-indulgence, a belief system that took years of entrepreneurship to unlearn.

Making more money than my parents felt like a betrayal, as if my success somehow highlighted their failure. It was another version of the same old pattern—my growth threatening the family system's equilibrium. But this time, I had the power to choose differently.

I knew I needed help to get out of my own way. I started working with business mentors to help me become a successful entrepreneur. One of them offered a tremendous insight about my money concerns during a two-day group intensive on leadership and mindset. In a room of 35 six- to eight-figure business owners, I stood at the microphone in the front of the room and shared the story of my only entrepreneurial role model—Tracy, my maternal grandmother.

The weight of this legacy was both powerful and poisonous. Tracy broke gender barriers when she moved to Washington, DC in 1940 to work for the US Department of Labor. This launched her lifetime commitment to helping disadvantaged people find jobs. While Debby and her sister were still in elementary school in the 1950s, Tracy established an employment agency in nearby Arlington, a radical move for a woman of that era. She hired two women to work for her, helping both men and women secure jobs at local companies.

Tracy was undeniably brilliant in business. Her agency thrived, eventually expanding to a second location in Alexandria, Virginia. In an era when most women didn't work outside the home, Tracy not only ran her own business but earned more than her journalist husband, a revolutionary achievement for the 1950s and '60s.

Around 1970, Tracy's business acumen reached new heights when she purchased the two-story building housing her employment agency. A few years later, she orchestrated a masterful deal, selling both the agency and building to her downstairs tenants for $1 million while maintaining control of the mortgage at 13 percent interest. In today's terms, that's equivalent to a $9 million sale—an extraordinary achievement for any business owner of that era, let alone a woman.

But success had a shadow side. Tracy, this pioneering business-woman, also sexually abused both me and Debby. In my subconscious, this created a toxic equation: financial abundance equaled sexual violation. Money became tangled with trauma, prosperity with pain.

Standing before this room of successful entrepreneurs, I laid bare this complicated legacy. I expected my mentor's response to follow the familiar script of sympathy: "Oh Emma, I'm so sorry that happened to you ... That must have been so hard." Instead, he delivered three words that would reshape my entire worldview: "You caused that."

The words hit me like a thunderbolt. He wasn't suggesting I invited the abuse or bore responsibility for Tracy's actions. His message was far more profound: I am the powerful creator of my reality. Everything that happens in our circumstances is neutral until we attribute meaning to it. I was the one who had forged the connection between financial success and sexual violation.

This revelation demanded a complete paradigm shift. To create a new reality, I had to acknowledge my role in creating my history of trauma and abuse, not as a victim or perpetrator but as a soul who chose this reality. I chose these parents and grandparents, these siblings, these experiences. Every moment of my journey—even the darkest ones—has shaped who I am today.

Everything that happened in my circumstances happened *for* me, not *to* me. I am not a victim of my childhood, nor am I merely a survivor. I am the powerful creator of my reality. Rather than crushing me, this responsibility gave me freedom. It allowed me to reclaim my power from the shadows of my past.

This lesson with my mentor became the key to unlocking my financial potential. I returned home from this two-day life-changing intensive and manifested my second $20,000 month. And I did it with nothing more than a basic website and no email list—proof that our internal barriers, once recognized and released, can no longer hold us back.

I was ecstatic! After years of wrestling with money trauma and generational patterns, I had finally broken through. Of course, I wanted to share this triumph with Kyle, my then-fiancé, the man I'd been living with for a couple of years. That evening, in our tiny apartment in a rundown, sprawling complex outside of Asheville, I eagerly waited for him to return from work. The apartment was a compromise. I always lived in houses before meeting him, but this seemed to be where he felt most comfortable, another sign of our differing aspirations that I had chosen to ignore.

When I shared my achievement, his reaction was immediate and I felt it viscerally. He declared that I was crazy to think I could consistently make $20,000 a month as a psychic and spiritual advisor and then he retreated to our bedroom, slamming the door behind him with a finality that echoed through our shared space. In that moment of rejection, I saw clearly how the patterns of my past—where success invited punishment—were repeating themselves.

That interaction with Kyle didn't happen *to* me, it happened *for* me—another divine lesson in recognizing when someone else's limitations threatened to become my own. I realized that he was unable to exist in a reality where my financial abundance was possible. His reaction wasn't just about money, it was about power, possibility, and the courage to step into one's full potential. Thank God he was so clear about his beliefs. I could see with crystal clarity how being in relationship with him was creating a ceiling over my growth.

In that moment, I closed the door on fearing money forever. I decided I was no longer willing to tolerate being around someone who was afraid of abundance, just as I had chosen to stop tolerating chaos from my family. After a couple of days of deep reflection, I ended my relationship with Kyle. This meant facing the daunting task of finding my own place to live, no small challenge for a self-employed spiritual advisor, even with my own limited liability corporation status and payroll. Most landlords saw my unconventional income stream as too risky, echoing the world's skepticism about my chosen path.

It took two months of persistent searching, but I finally found a place to lease—a 1,000-square-foot mountain cabin. The financial demands were steep: three months' rent upfront, plus a security deposit, plus three months of utilities in advance. Yet this massive financial outlay felt like an investment in my freedom—the price of no longer living with someone who couldn't abide creating money quickly and easily. It was a declaration of independence from the scarcity mindset that had shaped my childhood.

Staying with Kyle would have been the easier choice, the safe choice—the kind of compromise I had watched Debby make countless times. But I knew that choosing comfort over growth would slowly suffocate my potential, both financially and personally. Walking away taught me profound lessons about self-worth and the kind of love I deserved—love that could celebrate my success instead of fearing it, love that could expand with my growth instead of containing it.

My experience with Kyle became a master class in the Law of Attraction. The Universe, I learned, is constantly delivering people, events, and circumstances that match our energetic frequency. We "order" our reality through the broadcasting station of our predominant beliefs, sending signals into the cosmic field that then manifest in our physical experience. The Universe, in its infinite abundance, always responds to these signals, attempting to support our expansion and growth.

But mixed messages create static in this cosmic ordering system. When we simultaneously broadcast frequencies of desire and unworthiness, abundance and scarcity, the Universe cannot clearly tune in to our intentions. Ending things with Kyle wasn't just about leaving a relationship; it was about clearing the static from my spiritual signal. I finally declared to the Universe, with unmistakable clarity, the type of love I deserved, the relationship with money I desired, and the life I was ready to create.

I began to allow myself to desire everything, all at once—a radical departure from my childhood programming. Most of us have been conditioned to portion out our desires, to make them smaller, more "reasonable." We've learned to compartmentalize our dreams, believing we can have love or money, success or peace, but never all simultaneously. This limitation fascinated me. As humans, we possess the extraordinary power to create any reality we can imagine, yet we often hold ourselves back, constrained by fear, limited by the absence of role models, or terrified of confronting our own potential.

We live little lives and then justify them with big excuses. We give more airtime to our limitations than our possibilities, letting our fears speak louder than our dreams.

Debby and Dad were master practitioners of this limited thinking. There was always a ready excuse for why we couldn't afford dental care, medical treatment, new clothes, or other basic necessities. They saw themselves as victims of circumstance rather than creators of their reality, starring in a tragedy of their own writing. My brothers absorbed this mindset, becoming exceptional sufferers—as if hardship was our family's inheritance.

Yet, ironically, Debby's alters demonstrated the art of manifestation daily in our home. When something happened on the Outside, they switched to a different or better-equipped personality to handle the situation.

Debby changed who she was externally, shape-shifting her entire identity depending on what was happening in her environment. When reality became too harsh, she simply disappeared, letting another self emerge to weather the storm. It was her mind's desperate attempt at survival, splintering like a shattered mirror, with each piece reflecting a different version of protection. Over and over again, I watched this dance of creation and adaptation, though its purpose was survival rather than thriving.

The human condition gravitates toward sameness. Though we are the only species blessed with an intellect capable of conscious creation, we rarely use it to imagine new possibilities for ourselves. Our subconscious mind, that primitive guardian of survival, strives to keep us unchanged, interpreting any deviation from the familiar as a threat. Change equals danger in this ancient part of our brain, which would rather keep us safely suffering than risk the unknown of growth.

But I had learned from Debby's alters and my own journey that transformation is possible. Where Debby used her imagination to fragment, I learned to use mine to integrate. Where she created new personalities to escape reality, I created new possibilities to enhance it. This understanding became central to my trauma recovery work, teaching others that the same power that can splinter us can also make us whole.

After leaving Kyle, I fully immersed myself in teaching Universal Laws and the practice of manifestation. This wasn't just a career pivot—it was a declaration of sovereignty. In my work as a spiritual advisor and mentor, I began teaching a revolutionary truth: We are solely responsible for every thought, deed, decision, choice, and action we take. This responsibility isn't a burden; it's the key to our liberation.

Where Debby's personalities fractured responsibility into pieces, I learned to embrace it wholly. This became my pathway to healing trauma, not through endless processing or staying stuck in the story but through conscious creation. I realized that trauma recovery isn't just about surviving the past, it's about claiming the power to shape our future. This is how I learned to play full out in my life, to reach for my biggest desires despite circumstances that seemed to say "not possible."

I learned that identity itself is fluid, not in the fragmenting way of Debby's alters but in the expansive way of conscious evolution. I could be anything and anyone I desired to be, not by escaping reality but by creating it.

PART 7

EVOLUTION

CHAPTER TWENTY-NINE
JEFF

The secret to evolution is that you must align with a new truth about who you are and what you are truly capable of. You must *choose* to become the most complete version of yourself.

By 2019, five years after my breakup with Kyle and my decision to fully embrace manifestation, I thought I had created a pretty good life. I had transformed my spiritual advisory practice into a business that ranked in the top 2.5 percent of revenue-earning women-owned businesses. From those first $20,000 months in 2014 that Kyle couldn't comprehend, I had built something remarkable. But I had reached a plateau that felt uncomfortably familiar, another ceiling created by old beliefs still waiting to be examined.

I had what I thought was a beautiful home, though it was still a rental. I loved living in my mountain cabin, and I had cultivated what I considered a great community of friends. I even got a dog after I moved out on my own. Winston, my miniature dachshund puppy, was stubborn, lovable, super smart, and hysterical. He kept me company and showed me that I could be a mother to him without losing myself. From the outside, it looked like the perfect recovery story—the trauma-chaplain-turned-successful entrepreneur, helping others transform their lives while building a thriving business. But beneath this carefully constructed surface, there were still desires I hadn't allowed myself to fully claim.

The biggest unrealized desires were that I didn't have a loving, intimate relationship with someone who could celebrate my success instead of fearing it as Kyle had. And, despite my business success, I still didn't own my own home. The idea of owning a house stirred up a storm of childhood programming. I secretly wanted my own home, but deeply embedded messages about greed, worthiness, and what good people should and shouldn't want were tied up in it. In my childhood, material desires were painted as character flaws, signs of moral weakness. And I wanted a home I was proud of, that no one could take from me. These unmet wishes for a life partner and home weren't just dreams—they were reflections of where I still needed to heal, showing me exactly where scarcity thinking still gripped my heart. After all, how could I fully claim abundance when part of me still believed I didn't deserve it?

The irony wasn't lost on me. Here I was, teaching others about manifestation and Universal Laws, helping them break through their own limitations, while still holding back parts of my own desires. Just as in 2014, when I had to choose between staying small with Kyle or stepping into my power, I was once again being called to expand. My journey from trauma to transformation wasn't complete—I was simply entering a new chapter.

In a moment of profound loneliness, I found myself drawn back to Adam—the same Adam who had shattered my sense of worth in my early thirties. Seventeen years had passed since we first met, and I convinced myself that time had been the great healer, that surely a man in his mid-forties would have outgrown his commitment phobia and the convenient shield of polyamory. We were both single, both older, both supposedly wiser. *Maybe*, I told myself, *this is destiny finally getting its timing right.*

Adam was a familiar pattern I hadn't yet learned to resist. He represented something intoxicating and dangerous: the fantasy that if I could just love someone enough, if I could just be patient enough, understanding enough, accommodating enough, I could transform them into the partner I needed them to be. It was the same magical thinking that had governed my childhood, the belief that my love could heal what was broken in others.

The truth I wasn't ready to face was that Adam had never been the problem. He had been consistent in his inability to commit, honest about his limitations, clear about what he could and couldn't offer. The problem was my willingness to accept crumbs and call them a feast, to mistake intensity for intimacy, to confuse the familiar ache of wanting someone unavailable with love itself.

Getting back together with Adam wasn't about him at all—it was about my own unhealed places, the parts of me that still believed I had to earn love through suffering, that still equated struggle with depth. It was about the girl who had spent her formative years trying to love her family into wholeness, applying that same futile strategy to romance.

This time, though, I learned the lesson more quickly. Because at forty-four, I finally understood that love shouldn't feel like a disease you can't cure—it should feel like coming home to yourself.

On paper, Adam possessed every quality I thought I wanted in a partner. He was successful, a fellow entrepreneur with similar values, also Quaker, highly educated, very liberal, and we enjoyed the same activities. He checked every box on my carefully curated list of desirable traits. What I couldn't see then was that my list itself was the problem—it was a blueprint for recreating trauma, not love.

Without conscious awareness, I had absorbed Debby's template for relationships during her romance with John in my teenage years. I was unconsciously recreating that same dynamic with Adam— desperately wanting him to save me and love me because he appeared capable of doing so. The parallels were eerie: Adam and John even resembled each other physically; both were consultants who struggled with working for others; and both carried themselves with an air of intellectual superiority that I mistook for strength.

Like Debby, Adam was a narcissist. Everything orbited around his needs, his schedule, his emotional weather. The moment I shifted focus from him to myself, he weaponized the word *selfish* against me—the same accusation that had silenced me throughout childhood.

I clung to the fantasy that my patience would eventually unlock his capacity for love. When he met me in Miami during a business event in early 2019, we had what felt like a breakthrough—magical days playing in the surf, sharing meals, reconnecting on a level that felt real. He visited Asheville several times, and we took long hikes while having serious conversations about reuniting and the possibility of my relocating to be with him.

But Adam, true to form, always found reasons why full commitment remained just out of reach. First, my dog became an issue—suddenly he wanted a cat, knowing Winston's hatred of felines. Then came the stipulations about moving in: I could join him, but not with my furniture or "too many" of my belongings. Each conversation introduced fresh obstacles, new conditions that made our future together feel increasingly conditional and small.

When I flew out for a long weekend to explore how his house might accommodate both of us, I told myself we were planning logistics. But really, I was conducting one final test—desperately hoping to find evidence that he was truly committed to loving me, not just the idea of having me available on his terms.

After picking me up from the airport, taking me to his house, and carrying my luggage in, Adam announced, "Look, I haven't had any time to exercise today. I'm going rollerblading by myself. I'll be home in four or five hours." Our visit was only scheduled to be for two days.

For the first time, I clearly saw his lack of commitment. In that moment, I decided that I would never be with someone who could not be present with me and love me completely. After crying for four hours while Adam rollerbladed, I told myself that I was done with compromising in love. I wasn't compromising in my business or in other areas of my life. *Why should I keep compromising in my love life?*

I said to myself what I always say in situations where I need a paradigm shift: *Fuck this shit. What else is possible?*

When he got back, I had my luggage ready at the door. I looked him in the eye and said, "I'm leaving, and you are never going to see or hear from me again." He tried to talk me out of it, which was his habit—he only moved toward me when I pulled away from him. But I stood my ground. And I never saw or heard from him again.

For a few months after ending it with Adam, I convinced myself that long-term relationships simply weren't in my DNA. Maybe I was built for business success, not romantic partnership—someone who could generate revenue but couldn't sustain love. It was easier to believe I was fundamentally flawed in matters of the heart than to examine why I kept choosing men who couldn't truly see me.

So I did what I always did when faced with emotional uncertainty: I threw myself into something I could control. I adopted another miniature dachshund puppy and named him Leroy. Suddenly my days were consumed with managing an eight-week-old ball of energy who had no concept of boundaries and Winston, my then three-year-old dachshund, who treated Leroy's arrival like a personal betrayal.

Winston had been my constant companion, my emotional support system through the chaos of building a business and navigating failed relationships. Now he spent his days in a state of perpetual indignation, growling at the tiny interloper and staging elaborate campaigns to reclaim his territory. He would physically push Leroy off my lap with the determination of a bouncer removing an unwelcome patron or wedge himself between us in their shared crate, shooting me looks that clearly communicated his displeasure with my life choices.

Watching Winston's jealousy and territorial behavior, I couldn't help but see the parallel to my own patterns. Here was a creature who had felt secure in his position as the sole recipient of my affection, now struggling to share space and love with another.

But there was something healing about navigating this canine drama. Unlike the human relationships that left me questioning my worth, this was a problem I could solve with patience, consistency, and clear boundaries. Slowly, I began to see that maybe the issue wasn't my capacity for love—maybe it was my willingness to accept relationships where love felt like a competition rather than a collaboration.

Finally, I was ready to consider a different type of relationship with a man. I was deep into the study of quantum physics at this time, getting my master's in metaphysics.

I knew that asking myself different questions was a good place to start if I was feeling blocked. I knew I was already manifesting because we're never really blocked with manifesting. I was just manifesting more of what I *didn't* want in a relationship instead of what I did want.

I called on the Universal Law of Polarity. The Law of Polarity exists in all physical and nonphysical things in the Universe. It is scientifically and spiritually proven. The law states that everything has an opposite side to it.

In other words, there are no halves in the Universe. You can't have the desire for something without the way for it to be manifest, to be available in your world at the same time. If you've identified a desire and don't yet have it, you're just in the negative aspect of the polarity.

You are already connected to the positive aspect. The negative and positive aspects are on the same spectrum. For example, with money the extreme negative is poverty, and the extreme positive is wealth or prosperity. With love, the extreme negative is neglect, and the extreme positive is adoration.

I started asking myself what I really, really wanted, what my fragile heart truly desired. What I desired was a husband, a true life partner who wanted to go all in on life *with* me, who was my equal, who would challenge me to grow and bring out the best in me, who would love me in all possible ways. I wanted the adoration, not the neglect.

I also asked myself what I was willing to stop doing in order to meet my husband. I realized I had to release the long list I had created about what I thought my husband was supposed to be like. So far that list had brought me several terrible relationships. If I was honest with myself, my traumatized child self-made that list, not my soul self. My thinking and current perspective were stopping me from having what I wanted. To manifest my husband, I had to change my thinking about what was possible.

The decision I made was to find my husband on a dating app. I put the Universe on serious notice and set a deadline of one week. I didn't worry about being a great girlfriend or wife. I didn't worry about healing all of my childhood wounds. I didn't worry about my track record of dating crappy men. I decided what I wanted. I knew it was available to me because my soul desire was so strong, and I did not give myself another option.

Jeff and I both swiped right forty-eight hours later. Ironically, he had also made the same decision and gave himself a deadline of three days on the same dating app. The icing on the cake? He narrowed his search to a three-mile radius from where he lived. That put me in range—we literally lived within minutes of each other.

I took Leroy to our first date. He was only four months old, and I didn't trust him to behave himself if left to his own devices at home. Jeff said I cheated by bringing Leroy because they immediately fell in love with each other.

We met at a brewery. Asheville has more breweries per capita than any other city in the United States, so this was a normal first-date location. We sat on the brewery's lawn in the late summer heat. Leroy was exploring everything. Jeff kept Leroy from eating inappropriate things and escaping down the hill into oncoming traffic as we talked.

I peppered Jeff with questions for three hours:

"What are you looking for in a relationship?"

"How do you feel about my being a psychic?"

"How much time do you spend with your family, and do you like them?"

These were probably not the best questions for me to ask during a first date, but I didn't want to invest time with someone who wasn't a match for me. Jeff answered every question, divulging a lot of information about himself, including his divorce from his wife of twenty years. I sat back and observed this guy being fully present in his life and with me.

Jeff shattered my carefully constructed relationship checklist. He was Catholic where I expected Quaker, Republican where I demanded Democrat, Southern where I had always gravitated toward Northern sensibilities. On paper, we were fundamentally incompatible—two people who should have politely disagreed over dinner and never seen each other again.

But Jeff introduced me to qualities I hadn't known to put on any list because I'd never experienced them. He brought care that didn't come with conditions, presence that didn't require me to perform, attention that felt like genuine curiosity rather than surveillance. His transparency was startling—no hidden agendas, no emotional land mines, no need to decode what he really meant. His loyalty wasn't something I had to earn or maintain through constant vigilance; it simply existed, steady and unshakeable.

What struck me most was his intelligence paired with quiet confidence rather than the intellectual arrogance I'd mistaken for strength in other men. Jeff knew what he knew without needing to prove it to anyone. He was capable in ways that felt foreign to me—not the performative competence of men trying to impress but the understated assurance of someone who simply handled what needed handling.

Where my father had been volatile and my exes had been unreliable, Jeff was steady. Where my success had threatened others, Jeff was genuinely proud. Where I had learned to brace for emotional storms, Jeff offered calm. He didn't need me to be smaller to feel bigger, didn't require my chaos to feel needed, didn't demand my brokenness to prove his worth.

With Jeff, I immediately understood that my relationship list had been designed to attract familiar dysfunction, not healthy love. I had been screening for surface compatibility while ignoring the deeper qualities that actually sustain a partnership. Jeff taught me that sometimes the best thing that can happen to your carefully laid plans is meeting someone who makes you throw them out entirely—not because they're wrong for you, but because they're so right that they expand your understanding of what's possible.

Jeff walked me to my car at the end of our date and texted me later to make sure I got home safely. For our second date, dinner at a restaurant, I couldn't get from my front door to my car because a snake was blocking my path. Not unusual in the mountains of Asheville. I called Jeff to tell him why I was running late, and he offered to come to my house and deal with the snake for me. I wasn't ready for him to know where I lived, but I appreciated that his first instinct was to protect me.

After a month of dating, we were with each other most of the time, both recognizing that this was a significant relationship for us. Jeff regularly brought food to my house, cooked for me, or helped me fix things around the house. We spent lots of time together exploring new-to-us hiking trails in Western North Carolina, and my dogs had already decided Jeff was their daddy.

Jeff started advising me in my business, offering his twenty-five years of experience as a director of sales and marketing for multiple corporations. I immediately began making a lot more money. With Jeff's guidance and support, I felt more stable as a business owner. My life and business evolved quickly with his support.

Less than six months after Jeff and I met, I got my period, and it wouldn't stop. I was bleeding profusely, going through a super-sized tampon every thirty minutes. I could barely leave the bathroom, let alone my house, because of the waterfall of blood exiting me. I went to my gynecologist, who examined me and said she felt fibroids in my uterus. She sent me for an ultrasound and MRI. Both confirmed massive fibroids.

It was March of 2020, and we had just gone into the first COVID-19 lockdown.

The hospital is only open for emergent surgeries. My surgery is scheduled within a month of diagnosis because it is harder and harder for me to breathe with each passing day. The fibroids are pushing against my lungs. I appear six months pregnant. Everything hurts.

I've never had surgery. I've never stayed overnight in a hospital, and now I'm looking down the barrel of a gun in the form of significant surgery and three nights alone in the hospital. Because of lockdown restrictions, Jeff isn't allowed to visit. No one can hold my hand before or after the surgery. My only option is to rely on a team of strangers to help me navigate this.

Before my surgery, I ask for the chaplain on call to come visit and pray with me. She does. She looks tired and overworked but stays with me as long as I need, talking through my surgery and laying her hands on me while she prays. I recall the many times I did the same for patients in the surgery ward, people with the same fears and concerns I'm having.

The surgeon called Jeff with the results while I was still sedated. She was excited to tell him that they conducted a total hysterectomy, removing my uterus as well as both of my ovaries and my cervix. Going into the surgery we thought it would be just a laparoscopic hysterectomy, but the fibroids occupied my entire uterus and were also attached to my ovaries, so that wasn't possible. The surgeon told Jeff that the mass of fibroids looked like a giant alien and that it was one of the largest masses she'd ever removed in her career.

A sample was sent to a lab for testing, and the result was benign.

I finally woke up close to 10:00 p.m., ten hours after I was first sedated. A nurse handed me my cell phone so I could call Jeff. He told me the news. I cried with him on the phone, from relief that it was over but also because I had lost my womanhood in just a matter of hours. Jeff calmed me down and told me that I would get through this.

I spent most of the remaining two days in my hospital room relearning how to pee, because my body could not remember, and avoiding looking at the twelve-inch incision, stapled shut, that ran from the base of my pelvis to up above my belly button. I was on so many drugs that nothing hurt, so I had time to contemplate what had just happened to me.

Once the anesthesia wore off, I realized how smart my body is. It created a giant mass of everything that did not naturally belong inside of me, to be removed in one fell swoop. Energetically, it felt like the toxicity and trauma from my childhood was removed as well. The fibroids captured that all up too.

I never wanted children. I was clear on this from the time I got my period at eleven. I didn't want to perpetuate my lineage of bad seeds. On some level, I knew I wasn't capable of raising children and protecting them from the trauma of my family. When I was twelve, I told Debby I wanted a hysterectomy because I was already irritated by having my monthly period, and because I was that sure I didn't want children. Her reply was, "But of course you'll want to have children. All women do."

It turns out that I knew, even at that pubescent age, that I would never have children. Jeff, having already raised two children in his first marriage, didn't want more either.

With the hysterectomy, the toxicity was gone for good, and I am safe now. With his tender care of me as I recover from the surgery, Jeff showed me that it is possible to feel safe. My need to be a survivor also disappeared with the hysterectomy. With Jeff's love, I stepped into thriving, instead of just surviving.

I had entered the Evolution Phase, the final phase of trauma recovery that I now teach. In evolution, we become what we focus on. Our work becomes holding our focus on what we most desire amid chaos. That is our real work as humans. We must learn to process our trauma as we are living in it, as we are moving through it, and as we are transforming it. It's all happening, simultaneously, in real time.

In the Evolution Phase, we become the people who can live in *and* process trauma simultaneously. Healing doesn't stop with the relieving of pain. It continues beyond that, in our search for love. Love is the gateway to our evolution as humans and is how we process as we go. Jeff's love for me became my gateway.

After my hospital stay was over, Jeff picked me up and took me home. He already had my prescription medications from the pharmacy and comforting food made for dinner. He moved in with me for three weeks, taking care of me and my two dogs. The first night, Leroy had massive diarrhea and pooped all over Winston and the crate they both sleep in. Jeff bathed both dogs, washed the crate, and ran the dog bed and blankets through the laundry. By morning, it looked like nothing had happened. I slept through the whole thing, thanks to heavy drugs.

I was entirely incapable of doing anything for myself during this time, a combination of being too drugged up and not being able to get into and out of bed by myself because of the giant staples in my stomach. Jeff didn't complain. He just put his life on hold, stepped up, and took care of me. He showed me what it means to be loved and cared for fully.

Everything changed when Jeff came into my life. He brought an incredible amount of stability and safety with him. If my life were to be threatened, I knew with certainty that Jeff would kill that person with his bare hands without hesitation.

We met later in life, when I was forty-five and Jeff was fifty-one. It took me that many years to be ready to be fiercely loved and protected by him.

CHAPTER THIRTY

SAVED

Bryce's drug and alcohol abuse continued so intensely in the decade following his heroin overdose in 2009 that his brain disintegrated significantly. By 2020, he sounded and acted like a five-year-old, only able to engage in basic topics, with little to no short-term memory. He lived off government assistance and occasionally found work washing dishes. He had almost no contact with his children.

Bryce was an innocuous man with a generally good attitude about life. He never seemed put upon or upset that his life had turned out the way it had. I rarely heard him yell or get upset with anyone else.

This changed, though, when Debby 2 tried to get back into contact with me via email around the time I met Jeff. I wasn't having it. I told Debby 2 that she was a narcissist and that I didn't want to have anything to do with her. A few days later, out of the blue, Bryce sent me a message on Facebook. He wrote, "I am going to fucking kill you bitch."

Debby was his source for money, including funding his drug rehab programs. Since he was frequently hospitalized, Debby had continued as his medical power of attorney. She also financially supported his three children as Bryce was unable to support them, financially or otherwise.

I imagine that Bryce believes the only thing he can do to protect Debby is to kill me.

I understand this is his addiction talking, coupled with his inability to process complex thoughts or emotions. Bryce has come close to dying at least a dozen times in the past three decades, mostly the result of his pancreas and kidneys shutting

down. Some of his brushes with death were self-induced, others the side effect of too
many drugs in his system or the result of living on the streets and getting beat up.
Jeff, my always protector, tells me he will keep me safe from Bryce.
I don't take Bryce's threat personally, and I block him on Facebook.

Like me, Jeff reinvented himself. He left a twenty-year marriage and a lifetime in New Orleans, moving to Asheville without knowing anyone except his parents and brother. He made a life for himself here, and then we made a life together.

Jeff brought the capacity to love me completely and be utterly devoted to me and to our relationship. I had to say no to everything that wasn't serving me in previous relationships—men who couldn't reciprocate love, or make time for me, or proactively nurture our relationship—to receive the love Jeff wanted to give me.

At one point, maybe five months or so into dating, we were driving home from a beautiful new hike we had been on. I was feeling a little irritated by how much time we were spending together—I had a business to run, after all. Jeff had retired at forty-five, six years before we met, so he had a lot of free time.

I was driving, and I remember looking over at him and asking what he planned to do with his life. I thought that he needed to get a hobby or something. He said, "My plan is to spend as much time with you as possible and get to know you."

Before I could even think, I said, "That's the most ridiculous thing I've ever heard." I actually thought that Jeff's wanting to spend even more time with me and get to know me better was absurd.

I was terrified of being completely seen and loved. It was easier for me to be with someone who couldn't completely see me and who couldn't fully commit.

I now understand how amazing I am, and of course Jeff just wanted to be with me as much as possible. However, while we were dating, I was still learning to fully appreciate the magnitude of Jeff's love. Because he was always loving me. Whatever I wanted to do, he supported.

With Jeff, I also lost interest in my trauma symptoms. Revisiting them had begun to bore me. I became more interested in living life and being fully present. Jeff showed me there was a different way to live than simply existing in reaction to the past.

———————

Jeff and I spent about a year looking for a house or property where we would build our forever home.

I spent most of my adult life making very little money, either working on behalf of Quaker organizations that didn't pay well or working part time while also running my own business, which didn't make a lot of money in the early days. It wasn't until 2015 that my business really took off and I was able to start saving money toward my dream home.

I knew that Bryce was homeless during this year of our searching for a home. This knowledge fed my inner critic, who whispered: *Who am I to put my money toward an even nicer home than what I already have when Bryce is unhoused?* The guilt felt familiar, like an old sweater I should have outgrown but keep putting back on.

Bryce never asked me for money. Never asked for anything, really. It was a trait we learned early, watching Debby's alters punish any sign of need or want. But I didn't offer help either. I told myself, *With his constant drug use, he won't even need a home soon.* My thoughts were brutal, but they're how I justified my boundaries, my choice to prioritize my own needs after decades of being the family caretaker.

I pretend that I'm not being "selfish"—that loaded word Debby used to describe "bad people" who dared to take care of themselves. It's the same label she applied to Tracy, my grandmother, for her business success. I don't want to be bad. The irony isn't lost on me— here I am, a trauma recovery expert helping others claim their power, while wrestling with whether it's selfish to own my own home.

Jeff looks at me like I'm speaking an alien language when I voice these doubts. "People own homes, Emma. That is normal behavior." His matter-of-fact response highlights how deeply my childhood programming still runs, where basic self-care feels like betrayal and success feels like abandonment. The same mindset that once made choosing toilet paper paralyzing now makes choosing a home feel like a moral crisis.

Jeff comes from wealth. He has two parents who love him and have been married for fifty-five years. He comes from lots and lots of stability. He tells me it's normal to have conversations that don't involve trauma. It's normal to have needs. It's normal to buy a house and live in it.

Our house and property hunting started after the COVID-19 pandemic began in the spring of 2020. We spent nights and weekends driving around in communities, all within an hour's drive of Asheville. We went through every neighborhood and on every road possible in each of the areas we were considering.

Meanwhile, we continued our regular hikes on our favorite mountain, about thirty minutes outside of Asheville. We wanted to live on this mountain but couldn't see how it would be possible. Houses rarely came up for sale here because, well, it's gorgeous, and no one ever wants to leave it. Families have been on this mountain for generations.

We befriended a man who owned a store at the base of the mountain. One day we stopped in after a long hike, and he mentioned that his next-door neighbor might be thinking of selling her house, which was her vacation home. We intuitively knew this was the opening we'd been looking for. We immediately said we'd love to see the house.

At that moment, the caretaker of the vacation house walked into the store and offered to drive us up and show us the house. I believe that synchronicity happened with the Universe's support. We said yes, without hesitation.

The house was on top of the mountain, in a gated HOA with only eight houses on eighty-five acres. Driving into the HOA was like moving into a magical fairyland, full of rare plants and so many wild animals it was breathtaking. I made an offer on the house that day, and it was accepted.

The woman selling the house was ninety years old and lived hours away in Florida. She didn't want to use a real estate agent to sell the house and also didn't know how to do things like sign documents online. I Googled things like "How do you buy a house without an agent?" to accommodate her needs and expedite the sale.

I found a lawyer to draw up the paperwork for us. I walked the seller through how to print documents from her email and fax signed copies to me. A lot of hand-holding was involved, and I had a steep learning curve. I had never bought property, which was more complicated without an agent.

But I decided I could figure it out and make it happen. Even though I was nervous about the whole process, I believed I was capable of doing new things. I didn't give up because I had never done it before. I didn't give up because of the hurdles I had to overcome with the homeowner. Every single day, I kept deciding that this was something I could do.

Jeff and I acted immediately when we knew this property and house could be our forever home. We didn't hesitate. We didn't worry about where the money was going to come from. We didn't worry about not using an agent. We knew exactly what was inspired action versus uninspired action, which allowed us to be able to make decisions quickly and for more synchronicities to continue unfolding, such as getting married a month after the house was ours because we knew we wanted that as well. The ceremony was a quiet affair, attended by just Jeff's immediate family and my aunt and uncle, who joined via Zoom. A pandemic wedding, but perfect for us.

I closed on the property less than sixty days after we first saw it, paying the exact amount that I wanted to.

Our new home was a yellow Cape Cod-style house. Built in 1978, it had never been renovated and didn't have air-conditioning. It had a minuscule kitchen and bathroom, and the plumbing and electrical systems were old. We decided to gut it, strip it down to the studs, keep only the original pine flooring, double the size, and transform it into a modern mountain home.

My business was doing really well, but I didn't have an extra $400K lying around to spend. I had some active prospects but not enough for the money we needed immediately for the downpayment or the renovation, which was going to cost hundreds of thousands of dollars. I didn't want to dip into my savings for this. We also weren't willing to touch any of Jeff's retirement money.

Coming up with this much money in such a short amount of time was a lot of stress to put on a new marriage, but it was a pivotal moment for me in my manifesting process. I didn't yet know the "how," but I wasn't telling myself I had to learn the how before I could commit to buying this house and renovating it. This was such a great lesson in not having to be perfect at everything to manifest.

I didn't even know what I desired the house to look like, inside or out. We never had nice things in our childhood home. Our house was littered with dirty, hand-me-down furniture, polyester comforters for our beds, and mismatched sheets with holes in them. Many of our dishes and clothes were also hand-me-downs. We didn't go out and buy things for the house to make it nicer. That was never a priority. I was always embarrassed to have friends over. Creating a beautiful home was not something I was taught to do.

I'd barely even purchased my own furniture before. Designing an entire house felt daunting. My mother-in-law, Linda, who had built and designed multiple houses for her family, ended up teaching me everything I needed to know.

Jeff suggested I ask Linda for her help with designing the house. My reply was, "Why would she want to do that?" Because in my family of origin, no one helped.

I remembered calling Debby once when I was sixteen, having just recently purchased my own car. I was stranded in the middle of the road, three blocks away from our house, because my car ran out of gas en route to the gas station. I knocked on a neighbor's door, asking to use their phone to call my mother. Debby answered the phone, said, "It's not my problem that your car is out of gas. Find someone else to help you," and hung up. I asked to use the phone book and looked up the phone number for our next-door neighbors, hoping they might be able to help. They did, bringing a full gas can over immediately and filling up my tank enough to get me to the gas station. When I got home, Debby ignored me.

I am used to being alone and not getting help when I most need it.

Jeff says, "Because my mother loves you, and because family helps out. That is what family does. Helps." So I learned to receive help from Linda.

Linda generously goes with me to the cabinet vendor, where I say things like, "I like the color gray." Linda turns this into a cool gray modern cabinet with sleek black hardware.

The countertop vendor is a similar conversation. When the vendor says that marble is very popular for new homes, I reply with, "I can't have an emotional relationship with marble." This results in getting dark gray carbonite counters for the kitchen and laundry room, and granite counters for the bathroom that resemble the natural stone found in our mountain, creating a beautiful tie-in between the outdoors and the indoors.

The tile vendor is the hardest for me because she has approximately 3,000 samples to choose from. I pick out one floor tile that I feel I can have an emotional relationship with—it's really the only thing I can relate to. Two hours later, Linda has done her magic, and we have all of the tile for the entire house selected. And it's perfect. I love everything about what we picked out for the house.

This was a huge shift for me—from not being allowed to even have desires as a child to over two decades of being an entrepreneur, learning how to have desires in my own business, and then to finally going all in with claiming my desires for a husband and a built-for-me home. I was quickly learning that it was safe for me personally to have desires and for them to manifest rapidly.

In the week following my signing the offer for the house, securing the lawyer to help with the paperwork, and beginning the search for a general contractor, my business generated $147K.

The money began pouring in. Some clients decided to renew, and others I hadn't heard from in years reached out to me. Some were brand-new. They all wanted to start working with me immediately, and many of them paid in full for their services.

The money continued to show up, always just in time for the $20,000 checks I was writing to vendors every other week for nine months to get the house built quickly.

We were able to obtain all the necessary supplies on time, despite the three- to six-month pandemic delays for items ranging from lumber to appliances, because we consistently took action toward our goals as soon as opportunities presented themselves. This is the person I became when I released my childhood trauma by becoming fully responsible for it and for my own freedom—the person who kept saying yes.

This commitment created the right opportunities for the house to be built in an extremely short amount of time during the pandemic and for the extra $400K we needed for renovations. Most people fail to identify the exact opportunities that will bring them what they most desire. They let their fear or their ego get in the way and they either miss the opportunities or are so busy acting in the wrong direction that the right opportunities don't come to them.

While I was excited about building my dream house, with my dream husband, on our favorite mountain, it wasn't all rainbows and unicorns. I was also downright terrified. I reminded myself over and over again that it was safe to have everything I wanted in a home, but part of me felt like building this house would erase my history and the values my parents taught me, that I was dishonoring my family by creating such a beautiful home full of shiny new things.

This luxury house, which I primarily paid for in cash, is a betrayal. I am committing treason.

In the past, the terror I was feeling would have shut me down. I would have told myself that my dream was too big and that it was too much of a financial and logistical risk to make. I would have said to myself that my desire was inappropriate and unsafe. But with Jeff and Linda's help, I leaned in and figured out exactly what I wanted and built our dream house without cutting any corners.

Debby somehow found out that I got married and reached out via email, wanting to connect. I had my email account set up so that any messages from her went into a special folder instead of my inbox. I didn't see her message for a few weeks. And then I sat on it for a while. Eventually, I let my guard down.

I convince myself that it's been a dozen years since I ended my relationship with my family, and that perhaps in those years Debby has grown and evolved. Maybe she isn't a narcissist anymore. Maybe now she remembers that she did have alters. Maybe she'll acknowledge the hell of my childhood, or at least acknowledge me. I write back, telling her about Jeff and that we are building a house together, wondering if maybe this time she can be a mother to me and celebrate my marriage and new life with me. She asks what she can do to help.

I am genuinely shocked. Jeff and I have multiple conversations about how to respond. Debby rarely volunteers support, especially unsolicited. I don't know whether to be suspicious of this or grateful that she is being generous. Finally deciding to take her at her word, I tell her that I'd love to have financial help with covering the cost of moving into the new house in a few months. She asks how much I need. "$3,000," I write, thinking there is no way in hell she will give me any money. All of her money has always gone to my brothers or her grandchildren, not to me.

Debby sends me a check for $3,000.

A month later, out of the blue, I got a text message from Alex telling me Edward had been in the hospital all week.

This was very unusual. Bryce was always the one in the hospital.

It's 5:00 p.m. on a Thursday in late October. I've had a busy week serving clients and meeting with our contractor for the fifth time in seven days to decide on yet another thing about the house. I am flat out exhausted, as we're six months into this house build and I'm having the busiest and most lucrative year of my business to date.

I've just finished my client calls for the day. Jeff is making dinner in the tiny kitchen of my two-bedroom rental cabin—my home for the past five years and now partly Jeff's since our June wedding. He still spends four nights a week at his parents' house, helping his mom care for his father, who has advanced Alzheimer's. I respect their family-first values, though they feel foreign to me. I always thought the point of family was to survive them and leave.

Jeff joins me on our dark grey L-shaped couch, our first joint furniture purchase. We sit at opposite ends of the sofa, the oversized stone fireplace commanding the wall before us—too grand for this tiny cabin but stunning, nonetheless. Between us, Winston and Leroy maintain their evening ritual. At precisely 5:01, Leroy's whimper and Winston's pleading paw remind us that some decisions, like dinnertime, require no deliberation at all.

I text Alex back, anxious to know more, but he provides very few details, uncommon for him as he's always the first to bring up bad news. I begin shaking and can't get warm. I know something is very, very wrong. I don't feel like I can handle a conversation quite yet, not without knowing the full context of what I'm stepping into.

I text Debby, even though I've only spoken to her a couple of times in the past twelve years. She doesn't respond.

Through Alex, the pieces eventually start coming together. He tells me that Edward's alcohol and drug use have gotten progressively worse over the past year, that Edward has been an alcoholic for at least twenty of his thirty-five years. This is the first I'm learning about any drug use, although this has probably been going on for years as well.

Alex told me that Edward was hospitalized four days ago and diagnosed with Stage 4 liver cirrhosis. He had stopped eating food almost a month before that and had only been consuming alcohol and drugs. His body had shut down, and he went from erratic, hysterical behavior to a comatose state. This afternoon, the medical team told Debby that Edward needs to go on hospice service.

I hadn't seen Edward in five years. His behavior was erratic during our last visit, and I couldn't even figure out how to have a conversation with him. He was unrecognizable to me.

It's now 6:00 p.m. I tell Jeff I'm going to pack a bag and drive from Asheville to Manassas, Virginia, about eight hours away, where Edward is hospitalized. Jeff's face shifts from concern to gentle resistance, the way it does when he sees me falling back into old family patterns. He tries to talk me out of driving all night, suggesting I wait until morning or "until I come to my senses"—his diplomatic way of saying he sees me slipping into the caretaker role I've worked so hard to leave behind.

Despite having never met any of them, Jeff is not a fan of my family. He's heard enough stories about Debby's personalities and witnessed enough of my healing journey to recognize when old trauma responses are being triggered. Unlike Kyle, my former fiancé, who feared my success, Jeff fears my regression—not for his sake but for mine. He's become my advocate in ways I never learned to be for myself, standing guard against the gravitational pull of family chaos that has defined so much of my life.

Knowing my husband is right, I remain glued to the sofa for the next two hours, unable to function. At 8:30 p.m., Alex texts to say Edward is dead. He was alone when it happened. Debby was by his side the entire time he was hospitalized, up until an hour before he died. She then mysteriously decided that she had to drive home before it got too dark. This tracks with Debby's capacity to only exist for her own needs. Her child has been killing himself, and is now taking his last breaths, and she is nowhere to be found.

Thus repeated our family pattern of death by suicide. Just like Dad, Edward literally drank and drugged himself to death after years of addiction.

I did not attend Edward's memorial. I couldn't. The thought of being around Debby 2, whose narcissism sucks up all the air in the room, was unbearable. She would have demanded we all be captive to her voice, agenda, and interpretation of reality, just as she had throughout our childhood. She would have made Edward's death about her pain, her loss, and her grief while I sat there, holding the weight of a different kind of mourning.

Instead, I spent the next six months crying and privately grieving the loss of my brother, who was also my child. I had raised Edward from birth, changing his diapers, making his bottles, and soothing his nightmares while Debby's alters cycled through their daily drama and Dad was lost in alcohol. Now, in death as in life, I mothered him in my own way, grieving him in private, protecting our truth from Debby's distortions. Debby performed her grief for an audience. I privately carry the singular pain of losing both a brother and a child I had raised as my own.

Edward never found his way out of our family's labyrinth of trauma. His death haunts me, not just as a failure of my protection but as a mirror reflecting the divergent paths two siblings can take when navigating the same toxic waters.

In thinking back on our childhood, I realize that I had an almost stubborn determination to live fully, to find meaning beyond mere survival by discovering a sense of purpose and following the path God laid before me. Edward didn't. His surrender to our family's dysfunction is a cruel reminder of how close I came to losing my own battle, how that innate will to live made all the difference between transcendence and tragedy.

His death serves as both wound and wisdom, teaching me that survival isn't just about strength—it's also about that mysterious inner light that either burns or doesn't, that inexplicable force that makes some of us fight while others fade.

CHAPTER THIRTY-ONE
CRUCIFIXION

About a year after Edward died, Alex called me out of the blue and announced that he was planning on ending his life. He had concocted a noble exit for himself, believing he would be doing everyone around him a favor by dying.

Alex is now forty, has never married, and has been alone for most of his adult life. After years of suffering with skin issues, he recently has been diagnosed with an inflammatory skin condition called hidradenitis suppurativa, which causes painful bumps, boils, and tunnels under the skin. It is not fatal. To effectively manage this condition, he was told he can no longer abuse drugs and alcohol and must eat a restrictive diet. He will need constant medication to manage infections and occasionally have minor surgery on his skin. With this diagnosis, and the continuous pain in his body, Alex feels that his life isn't worth living anymore.

I'm genuinely trying to have compassion for him, but I am irritated by this conversation. I'm in constant pain from the chronic Lyme disease that I've had for a dozen years, which I contracted from a tick when I was living and working at the Quaker center outside of Philadelphia. Like Alex, I too must manage my diet, alcohol consumption, sleep, and stress because so many things can trigger a Lyme disease flare-up. I take thirty supplements a day to strengthen my immune system, which keeps the symptoms at bay. The side effects I live with are exhaustion, insomnia, brain fog, pain all over my body, and migraines.

I know all of these things and have taken the path of 100 percent responsibility for my life and my body.

Everyone with a chronic health condition has a choice of how they are going to deal with it, whether to let it define them or not. I have chosen the path of living with my chronic condition, not dying because of it. I have made a life for myself, despite what's going on with my body.

I haven't chosen the path of alcohol or drug addiction or suicidal ideation like everyone else in my family.

I am a successful business owner and the primary breadwinner in my family. Alex doesn't work and lives off friends' support. One friend lets him live for free in one of his rental houses; others supply him with food and alcohol. Alex says it's "pride" that keeps him from using government assistance. Alex thinks of himself as "better than" Bryce, who does live on government assistance as part of his latest drug rehabilitation program.

I am sick of my family refusing to take responsibility for themselves and their lives. They have chosen delusion as their preferred method of self-preservation, and Alex has just taken his to the next level.

Sitting in my home office, looking out the window at the beautiful mountain and woods behind our recently completed house, feeling incredibly grateful for where Jeff and I live and the life I have built, I say to Alex, "Look... you have always been one foot in and one foot out of this world. You are forty years old, and you need to decide once and for all if you're in this game of life or not. Whatever you decide to do I will accept, but right now you are taking the coward's way out, just like Dad and Edward did. This is your one precious life. I hope you choose to live it. I love you, but I can't be in this fantasy with you."

If Debbie Sue was still around, I imagine she would have said something similar to him. Sometimes you just gotta confront craziness with some straight talk.

On a hot July afternoon in 2024, nearly two years later, I received another call from Alex, with the same description of his skin condition. This time he added that he has been using alcohol to self-medicate, because he "doesn't want to become one of those people addicted to opiates." It seems his delusion has advanced.

Debby 2 had recently visited him for a week, in an attempt to wean him off of the "Demon Rum," as she calls it. Probably, knowing her, Alex's consumption is inappropriate because it begins the moment he wakes up. Debby 2, like Frank and all the other drinkers in our family, waits until the respectable hour of 5:00 p.m. to have her first drink of the day. In Debby 2's mind, her glass (or glasses) of wine every night is totally different from Alex's all-day consumption of liquor.

Alex announces, once again, that he is going to end his own life. Only this time he has a plan. In three days' time he will walk into the woods with a noose and a cocktail of drugs he has already acquired. He will take the cocktail and then hang himself from a tree in case the drugs don't finish the job.

I am glad I have my headset on because this confession has caused my arm to lose the ability to hold my cell phone. I don't want to be Alex's confessor, the role he has obviously chosen for me.

I ask him who else knows about this plan. "Six people, including you. Not Debby, of course." We both know she is incapable of facing any truth about her children. I am not surprised that Alex hasn't told her. The weight of his confession lessens once I know I am not the only one holding this suicide plan.

Alex continues to rationalize his decision to die, citing "the state of the modern world," "the decline of our society," and "the bourgeois." The last rationale is my personal favorite, although, when confronted, Alex is not able to provide further explanation. He adores the pseudo-intellectual world he has created for himself. But his intellectualism, like his disease, is only skin deep. I just can't with his use of the English language to exalt his suicide plan.

"Are you calling to ask for my permission, or my blessing, or just as an FYI?" I ask.

"An FYI, but I'm cool if you give your permission and your blessing."

It is cruel of Alex to call and put this on me.

I've had so many conversations with Alex about death, the meaning of it, and when (and if) it is warranted. He was raised Quaker, and although he rarely attends Quaker meetings as an adult, he still considers himself to be practicing.

Liberal Quakers, like us, believe there is life after death. We don't believe in heaven and hell per se. Many of us do think that there is a reckoning at the end of one's life where you are invited to look back at your life and consider your life choices and how you might want to do things differently in your next life, if you have one. Alex and I don't discuss this theology during our conversation, but I know he believes these things.

Forty-five minutes into our conversation, Alex is itching to get off the phone. I hear someone talking in the background and the rustling of a paper bag. I suspect a liquor delivery. Alex says, "Um, Em. I gotta go." He signs off quickly, telling me he loves me. I say, "I love you too, Ax," my nickname for him since he was little and couldn't pronounce Alex, only Ax.

It's only 2:00 p.m., but I've finished with my coaching clients for the day, and I feel like I've been emotionally sandblasted after the conversation with Alex. His delusions always send me spiraling, not just because of what he says but because of how quickly they transport me back to the chaos of our childhood, where reality was always negotiable and truth was whatever the most volatile person in the room declared it to be.

I want to disappear from my own skin, to find some way to silence the familiar anxiety that's now thrumming through my nervous system. But unlike my family members, I lack the addictive personality that might offer easy escape routes. My tolerance for alcohol is embarrassingly low, and drugs have never held appeal—my body too sensitive, my control too precious to surrender.

Still, today feels different. The weight of maintaining boundaries with my family while building a business around healing feels impossibly heavy. Maybe, I think, alcohol can be my temporary ally in this moment.

Since I work from home, I can easily access our kitchen and bed. I pour myself a gigantic glass of white wine and add ice cubes to make it cold. I rarely drink, so we don't have any chilled wine in the fridge. I crawl into the king-sized bed I share with Jeff and pull the covers up to my neck, wondering if I should have brought a straw with me for easier sipping.

Jeff comes in and reminds me that alcohol gives me headaches (I already know this) and that I'm going to regret this decision in the morning (he's right, I will). He asks if I want to talk about the conversation I just had with Alex (I don't). I know he is being kind and caring, but I just want to be left alone in my bed of misery.

Alone in the cool bedroom, staring out the French doors at the trees behind our house, I wonder when I will stop being so emotional every single time I talk to one of my family members. I berate myself for allowing their delusions to impact *me so much. I try coaching myself through this internal self-talk like I would with one of my clients coming to me upset about a family dynamic.*

It doesn't work. I raise my head off my pillow for another sip of the wine. I should have grabbed a straw.

I let myself cry and feel sorry for myself and worry about Alex. I get angry and yell at him in my head.

"What the fuck is wrong with you, Alex? Why can't you just fucking pull your shit together? You didn't have it as bad as I did growing up. I protected you. Why can't you even try to live?"

I watch bad TV. Eventually I fall asleep.

Four hours later, I crawl out of bed and walk down the hall into the kitchen. Jeff has made dinner, a healthy, organic, balanced meal, the type of food we always have at home because my diet is restricted to control Lyme disease flare-ups and because we are both watching our weight. I eat some to balance out the toxic alcohol in my system. I already have a headache. I am already regretting my choice to drink.

Then we talk about Alex. Our conversation continues on and off for the next seventy-two hours, until the day Alex told me he had set to end his life.

"Do I drive five hours and try to find Alex and stop him from doing this?" I ask Jeff and myself.

"Do I notify Debby or the police?"

"How do I figure out where he lives?"

"Should I have another conversation with him?"

"What else do I need to tell him, or need to ask him, in case he actually goes through with it this time?"

I keep feeling the old pull of responsibility, the familiar weight of being the family savior. Alex wouldn't have called me if he didn't want me to intervene, right? Jeff and I get into several arguments about this. He sees what I can't, that I'm being drawn back into the vortex of family trauma. He doesn't want me to chase after Alex, knowing how this pattern played out before with Edward.

I can't separate my emotions from my conditioning. I am about to lose yet another brother. I am angry and drowning in guilt that Alex's delusions have gotten this bad in my absence. The same questions that haunted me after Edward's death now echo through my sleepless nights: Why didn't I stay and protect him? Why didn't I keep him from getting this bad?

The cost of saving myself, of breaking free from chaos, of building a successful business, of finding healthy love with Jeff, seems to be losing all of my brothers to drugs and alcohol. One life for the price of three. A sucker punch to my soul that makes me question everything I've taught others about trauma recovery and transformation.

I don't sleep for three days, caught in an emotional crisis that feels both new and anciently familiar. My old way of operating—rushing in to fix everything, being the family's designated rescuer—is no longer accessible to me. It's as if my healing journey has locked that door forever. All of the emotions I couldn't feel as a child, all the grief and rage and helplessness I suppressed, come rushing back over these seventy-two hours. They render me paralyzed, not with indecision but with the profound recognition that saving myself meant letting go, even if letting go felt like betrayal.

Jeff, always the voice of reason, reminds me that Alex has wanted to end his life for thirty-five years. This is his biggest desire in life. If he wants to die, he is going to die.

Jeff is right. I hate that he is right. Alex wants to die.

Knowing in advance that Alex is planning on ending his life feels harder than finding out, only hours before his death, that Edward's was coming to an end. The anticipation is excruciating. I am a witness to a crime that has not yet been committed.

I text Alex on his appointed death date, finally ready to tell him that I do not give my permission. I do not bless this ultimate act of self-sabotage.

I send him a text message: "Just checking in. How are you doing today?"

Alex: "I persist. It was so lovely speaking with you the other day. In case you didn't know, even if I didn't have to love you as a sibling, I would just love you as a whole ass person."

Me: "Oh my gosh, Alex, thank you so much. I feel the same."

Alex: "Mwah."

Then I let it go. I didn't bring up his request for my permission or blessing. I didn't go to visit him. I waited. Weeks passed. I tried my best not to think about it, hoping this was just another one of Alex's attempts to do something he never follows through with. I shoved down the aching in my heart for Alex to be someone other than who he has always been.

My entire life, I have been surrounded by people who want to die. Just like Bryce trying to die since he was twelve. Just like Edward dying by suicide at age thirty-five. Just like our father dying by suicide at age forty-eight. Just like Debby, who began trying to die when she was fifteen.

I am still learning how to attend to the gulf of sadness that exists between my brothers and me. Everything I wanted for them, as their older sister and mother. Everything they did not claim as their own.

The men they did not become. The legacies they did not create.

Alex died on a Friday morning in early August, the first sunny and remarkably cool day we had had in a month. Three weeks after our last conversation, I had almost given up the idea that he would follow through with his suicide plan. Almost… That word contains all the difference between hope and devastation.

That afternoon, I received a phone call from a detective, who told me he found my name and number in a database the police can access that traces family relations. This slightly creeped me out. Just like with our father, I was listed as next of kin instead of Debby, a bureaucratic acknowledgment of the reality I had lived since childhood.

I do not want to be in this database. Being next of kin means being the one who makes final decisions, just as I made daily decisions throughout my childhood.

It is an active investigation, the detective says, so he can't tell me where or how Alex died. He does let it slip that he has only been dead for a few hours and that a stranger found him.

I ask all of the right questions, my voice steady and professional—muscle memory from my years as a trauma chaplain. The irony isn't lost on me: I spent years helping others navigate sudden loss in emergency rooms and trauma centers, and now I'm on the other side of that conversation, using that same training to manage my own brother's death.

"*What is the phone number for the morgue and the medical examiner?*"

"*When can the medical examiner examine the body?*"

"*What is the police case number?*"

"*What is the name and number of the department that handles death certificates?*"

"*How long until a funeral home needs to pick up the body?*"

I am holding it together. I am a professional. I know how to handle this. I will cry later when I am done with this conversation, when I am with my husband and safe.

It's Friday afternoon, and the medical examiner can't view Alex's body until possibly Monday to officially declare him dead and determine the cause of death.

So I spend the weekend in limbo with a body that has not officially been declared dead. I startle awake at night throughout that weekend with the image of Alex hanging lifeless from a tree. I know he is not at rest. I can feel he hasn't yet figured out that he is dead.

I contacted Debby to tell her about Alex's passing. I didn't want to speak to her because our last conversation was too painful. But text or email felt cruel. I knew she would not be able to hear the news directly from a detective—that would be too much for her.

I called Debby, not as her daughter but as a trauma chaplain. That helped. Before sharing the news, I asked if she had someone to be with her in person. She said yes. I gave her only the basics of what I knew, nothing about the drug cocktail or the hanging, just that he was gone, it was definitely a suicide, and she needed to locate a funeral home near where Alex had been living.

"Can you call Susan?" Debby asks. "I just can't bring myself to tell her that Alex died."

"I haven't spoken to Susan in twenty years. I am not comfortable doing that."

Debby is the parent. This is her responsibility. Years ago, I decided I would no longer play Debby's game of making me the responsible one.

I get off the phone with Debby and spend the next month barely able to function. Alex's death hits me like a sucker punch. Even though I am not his mother, I have lost a child. Well-meaning friends orbit around Debby like concerned satellites, bearing cards and condolences for "the mother." They reach out to me, asking for her address and phone number. My grief becomes a footnote in their expressions of sympathy, just as it was with Edward's death. My loss, like my years of surrogate parenting, remains invisible—a shadow grief that no one knows how to acknowledge.

I keep dreaming of Alex, hanging lifeless from a tree. I am barely sleeping and am bursting into tears uncontrollably. They leak out of my eyes at inopportune moments—walking the dogs, between client calls, paying bills, and always when I am alone.

Jeff gets irritated with me. My grief has infiltrated our sex life and our regular schedule. I don't want to hang out with friends or go to the gym together or even watch TV with him after dinner. I don't want to work. I don't want to hear about what is going on for anyone else. I just want to be left in my misery. I deserve it. I must be alone to nurture and attend to it.

I do manage to go to yoga class a few times a week. Practicing breathing in and out, remembering to inhabit my body, calms my nervous system. It is the only thing that feels good to me.

I surrender to Savasana (corpse pose) over and over again. Not doing. Not being. Allowing.

During one restorative yoga class, my grief eventually shifted from the image of Alex's lifeless body hanging from a tree to an image of him when he was four

He is running through a field of sunflowers taller than him. Laughing with excitement, he is delighting in being hidden amongst such beauty.

My breath eventually found its way to my toes and then to other body parts—kneecaps, the small of my back, my heart, my throat, and the center of my forehead. It was August, and the yoga studio had no air-conditioning, so it was hot. The garage doors were wide open. Breeze carried the breath of life into our classroom and into me.

I became engulfed by my breath. A few weeks into this spiritual practice, everything in my body had become limber, except the middle of my back, where grief had taken up residence. I practiced breathing into my back.

While removing consciousness from my body in the stillness of Savasana, I meet my brothers and my father. I am in blank space with them, not an other world or heaven. Just blankness. Like being in outer space, but in a black hole. For three minutes I stop feeling anything, a welcome relief.

The restorative class teacher now invites me to return consciousness to my body. To inhabit it. To embody everything, including my grief. The back of my rib cage remains stiff.

On the drive home from that class, I passed by a man similar in age to Alex. Walking along the highway, he wore jeans and an unbuttoned, long-sleeved collared shirt, exposing his midriff. A giant black tattoo of a cross covers the expanse of his chest.

A living crucifixion.

I wonder, as the noose contracted around his neck, if Alex too believed that he was sacrificing himself.

CHAPTER THIRTY-TWO
CHURCHWOOD

In our last conversation, Alex told me that he didn't want to be a burden to anyone. Even the note he pinned to his body before he died began with "I'm sorry. Thanks for taking care of this..." and ended with, "Hope your life goes better than mine did, and good luck with the future." Even when facing death, Alex was firstly concerned about his impact on others, including whoever found him.

Bryce, on the other hand, never seemed concerned about his impact on our family. His addiction, whether he was sober or using, drove all his decisions and actions. Nothing else mattered.

When he was using, communication was impossible. When he was sober, he was emotionally vacant—a ghost walking through his own life. Either way, I couldn't reach him. He was just a blank space of a person.

Less than three months after Alex died, Bryce also died by suicide. He was forty-eight. At his death, his struggle with drug and alcohol addiction, including several overdoses, had lasted for nearly four decades. He had become estranged from his children over the fifteen years before that and was living in a government-supported apartment in Washington, DC, having just moved out of a halfway house. He had been sober for a year and a half, one of his longer stretches of sobriety, and was washing dishes for a living.

I got the call about Bryce from Mary Jane, a close friend of Debby's I hadn't spoken to in thirty years. Another sucker punch to the gut—the same visceral pain I felt with Alex, with Edward, with each brother-child I had raised while Debby's personalities danced their daily chaos. The last domino had fallen, and with it my carefully constructed professional composure shattered.

I break into a guttural, animal, fall-to-my-knees, hand-to-God cry for help. Not the controlled grief I once guided others through as a trauma chaplain but the raw, primal scream of a mother-sister losing her last surviving brother. All my training, all my healing work, all my teaching others about trauma recovery—none of it shields me from this moment. This is the cry of a teenage girl who once bathed, fed, and protected three little boys while their mother fractured into pieces and their father disappeared into bottles. This is the sound of final surrender.

Mary Jane tells me that Debby hadn't heard from Bryce for a few days, but instead of driving the three miles between her apartment and his to check on Bryce herself, Debby called law enforcement and asked for a welfare check. She must have known something bad had happened; she's always been intuitive like that. She's always conveniently not there when it matters most. She couldn't be there for me either, to alert me to Bryce's death. She hid behind a friend.

Bryce died two weeks after the hell of Hurricane Helene struck Western North Carolina and devastated our tiny community on September 26, 2024. The call from Mary Jane came less than twenty-four hours after my cell service was somewhat restored after being knocked out for those two weeks.

All the roads below our home were destroyed. We were trapped near the top of our mountain for two weeks and had no power for seventeen days. In a matter of hours, we were living in an apocalyptic state. We had neighbors who lost their homes and vehicles in massive mudslides or floods. In the aftermath, we barely had internet access, and most of our cell phones didn't work for the first month. I had to shut down my online business because it was impossible to run with no power or access. I began volunteering as the trauma chaplain for our small community of 300 people, and Jeff coordinated communications and supplies from the outside world for all of us.

Every day had become a primal exercise in survival, figuring out how to get food, attend to neighbors, protect our property. The hurricane stripped away all pretense, reducing life to its most basic elements. Just as I had done in childhood while managing Debby, I found myself once again orchestrating survival for others. In the midst of this, I got the news about Bryce. The icing on the proverbial cake was that he died on Debby's 75th birthday. It was a final act of defiance against the mother who had fractured into pieces throughout our childhood.

My brain churned with a familiar anger. *How dare Bryce, once again, make this about him?* So much of my life had been about his addiction––the endless cycles of crisis and recovery, hope and disappointment. I was just beginning to process Alex's death, learning to navigate the world with yet another brother-shaped hole in it, when Hurricane Helene turned everything upside down. Now, as I struggled to lead my community through devastating loss, Bryce chose this moment to follow our brothers into oblivion.

The parallels were brutal—managing community trauma while processing personal grief, just as I had done throughout childhood, caring for my brothers while managing Debby's chaos. Once again, I was caught between being the strong one and falling apart, between helping others survive and mourning my own losses. The hurricane's destruction mirrored the devastation in my heart, both leaving me to rebuild from ruins.

I shut down my business for three months following the hurricane because of too many disasters on top of one another. Even with all of my training in trauma recovery, all of my experience attending to my own trauma and helping others to attend to theirs, this much loss and devastation was too much. I needed to take a beat and recover myself. Most of my clients were incredibly understanding of this, and I was able to deeply care for myself and our community during this time.

I had never taken a significant break like this in any of my businesses. It was a massive risk for me, but it also felt like a signal from God. I was compelled to take this risk, knowing that it would take me to something greater, even though I had no idea what that was at the time. God's voice in the center of my forehead confirmed this decision.

Immediately after the hurricane, I started writing daily Facebook posts about what was happening in our small community, and this became my trauma recovery. I wrote my way through the apocalypse, thinking that if I could help make sense of it to the outside world, then I could make sense of it for myself too. It worked. Forty days of daily posts, followed by intermittent posts every five to ten days, became my therapeutic recovery. I wrote my way into healing.

This writing became one of the first books released about Hurricane Helene. *The Deep End of Hope in the Wake of Hurricane Helene* is a story of survival and transformation in the midst of horrendous devastation. It shows how walking with trauma without it defining you is possible. In the book, I talk about how to use gratitude and love to fortify yourself so you can become someone who thrives on the other side of trauma instead of merely suffering through it or surviving it.

My only communication with Debby during this time was when she texted me the notification of Bryce's memorial a few weeks after he died. Just a square-sized image with his name, birth and death dates, his picture, and the date, time, and location of his memorial. A calming blue background held the information together in a sorrowful yet appropriate way. Nothing else was included with the image.

I immediately noticed that Bryce's last name was misspelled: *Churchwood* instead of *Churchman*. This is the third of Debby's three sons for whom she organized a memorial in the last three years. That is too much death, and too much life, to memorialize. Not catching the misspelling of his last name was a trauma response. Details are one of the first things to go. The mind sees what it wants to see instead of what is actually there.

Bryce's picture hits me like a prophecy fulfilled. He is staring back through time, wearing our father's face like an inherited curse. The puffy rings beneath his eyes tell the same story of bottles emptied and dreams drowned, a genetic legacy written in bloated flesh and broken capillaries. His eyes hold that familiar haunted look—the one I saw in Dad's gaze countless times—a map of loss etched by missed exits and wrong turns, each lost opportunity adding another layer of grief to their shared gaze.

His untrimmed beard, just beginning to silver, frames a mouth that's forgotten how to smile. The mirror image is so complete it burns: Father and son, each extinguished at forty-eight, as if even their expiration dates were predetermined by some cruel genetic timer.

But my mind rebelled against this final image, desperately reaching back through decades to grab hold of a different Bryce: my little brother sprawled on his bedroom floor, orchestrating elaborate adventures with toy cars across a landscape of wooden blocks. In that treasured memory, his voice rose and fell with *vroom-vroom* sound effects, his imagination transforming our troubled home into race-tracks and highways. That boy lived in a world of his own making, where toy cars could outrun destiny, and wooden blocks could build foundations strong enough to hold any weight.

The contrast between these two Bryces—the child lost in innocent play and the man who followed our father's footsteps into an early grave—split my heart along fault lines of what was and what could have been. In the end, both Dad and Bryce chose the same escape route, leaving behind identical portraits of pain, while I clutch at memories of a brother who once knew how to play, how to dream, how to live.

I knew the ending of Bryce's life before it was even written. He knew it too. He called me the day Alex died, two and a half months ago, and was startlingly honest with me during that ten-minute conversation.

Bryce: "I don't blame you [for not wanting to be a part of our family]. I know you are protecting yourself. It's okay. I'm glad you have a husband and a happy life."

Alex told me the same thing in our last conversation, three weeks before he died.

Me: "Thank you, Bryce. I appreciate hearing that. I love you, but I can't be a part of Debby's delusions. That's why I distanced myself."

Bryce: "You and Alex had it much harder than me. You stayed. I escaped through drugs." I'm shocked by this revelation. I always thought Bryce had it the worst because he took the brunt of the physical abuse from Dad and because he started using at such a young age.

Me: "Bryce, you had it really hard, too. I'm so sorry Dad was so awful to you."

Bryce: "I thought I would be the first one of us to die."

Me: "I did, too."

Me: "I'm here for you. Reach out anytime if you need help."

Bryce: "Okay."

I never heard from him again.

I knew the drugs and alcohol would kill Bryce after the first time he overdosed when he was twelve and I found him naked and strung out on the floor of his bedroom before school. Even so, when I learned he died from an overdose, my first thought was of the conversation we had only a few months ago. *Did my comment tip him over the edge? After all this time, was he waiting for me to tell him that I knew he would die?* That is one detail that I will never know. I added it to my catalog of regrets.

All of my brothers, and our father, chose their own forms of resolution with death. I disagreed with them, but that is the advantage we have as humans—to choose. This is what all of us do, ultimately—choose for ourselves the trajectory of our lives.

Even when circumstances seem to conspire to make us feel powerless, when the storms of life rage around us and through us, we retain an essential sovereignty: the power to choose our response. This isn't just positive thinking—it's practical resilience. When hurricanes tear through our carefully constructed plans, when trauma reshapes our landscape, when others' choices send ripples through our reality, we still hold the pen that writes our next chapter.

This sovereignty of response isn't about denying our pain or minimizing our challenges. Rather, it's about recognizing that within every moment of powerlessness lies a seed of power—the power to choose how we meet our circumstances, how we language our experience, how we navigate our way forward. It's the difference between "I can't handle this" and "I am handling this moment by moment," between being swept away by the current and learning to swim with intentional strokes.

Our greatest freedom lies in this space between stimulus and response—the freedom to transform trauma into resilience, crisis into capability, challenge into evolution.

I chose to continue to release my anger toward my family. Instead of feeling like a martyr, like I had sacrificed myself on the cross of Debby in order to save her and my brothers and to compensate for my father's absence, I let go my role of victim. I am not a victim of my family. I am not even a survivor, really. I am an old soul who came into this world to understand the underbelly of the human experience so I can help others heal and transform their own humanity. That is my role and purpose.

With my brothers' deaths, my anger toward each of my family members for the choices they made shifted even more to compassionate grace. I consciously chose to create resolution for myself because I saw that it was time for me to release my past and embrace my mission more fully.

Forgiveness doesn't always look like reconciliation. There will be no scene of Debby and me hugging it out, spending holidays together, or having mother-daughter dates. The myth of mandatory reconciliation has caused as much harm as healing in trauma recovery. While our culture often elevates reconciliation as the gold standard of forgiveness, this perspective can become another form of trauma— forcing survivors to shoulder the additional burden of mending bridges that others burned.

Forgiveness exists on a spectrum, with reconciliation being just one possible destination, not the required final stop. Sometimes, the most profound act of self-love is maintaining the boundaries that protect us from further harm. Sometimes, wisdom looks like acknowledging that a relationship can remain broken while we become whole.

Through my work with trauma survivors and my own journey navigating the complex web of relationships with my father's alcoholism and Debby's alters, I've learned that forgiveness can mean simply laying down the weight of resentment without picking up the task of relationship repair. It can mean releasing ourselves from the obligation to make things "right" with someone who hasn't demonstrated the capacity or willingness to do their own healing work.

True forgiveness might look like accepting that some doors are better left closed, that some bridges are better left uncrossed. It might mean choosing to direct our energy toward nurturing relationships that feed our resilience rather than depleting it in futile attempts to resurrect connections that compromise our well-being.

This isn't about holding grudges—it's about holding space for our healing, transforming "I should reconcile" into "I am choosing what serves my highest good." Sometimes, the most potent form of forgiveness is the quiet acknowledgment that we can release the past without recreating the conditions that caused our wounds.

I now know that I cannot heal a broken relationship with someone who is still broken. Broken plus more broken doesn't equal wholeness. For me, forgiveness looks like accepting that Debby will never be the mother I need her to be. It looks like finding mothering and family in other people. It looks like releasing her from any expectations I have about who I want her to be. It looks like finding other ways to live life outside of my family of origin.

I always thought I was normal for wanting to live life. But I've come to realize that I am the exception. Living is hard for so many people.

For decades, I mistook my will to live as unremarkable—as natural as breathing, as common as rainfall. But through my journey I've discovered that my innate drive toward life is rarer than I imagined. While others perfect the art of emotional surrender, I've always burned with an inexplicable pilot light that refuses to be extinguished.

Living, I've learned, is an act of profound courage for many. The simple act of choosing to fully inhabit each moment requires a strength that some spend lifetimes gathering. As F. Scott Fitzgerald wrote, "Vitality shows in not only the ability to persist but the ability to start over." This resonates deeply with my work in trauma recovery, where I daily witness the raw courage it takes to choose life after devastation.

My seemingly natural inclination toward living—not just surviving, but truly living—has become one of my most valuable tools in helping others transform their trauma language into resilience language. This vitality isn't just about persistence—it's about the audacity to begin again, to believe in new possibilities even when the evidence suggests otherwise. It's the same force that drove me to become a trauma recovery expert, to help others find their way back to fully living, to transform wellness into true resilience.

My father couldn't start over after he and Debby divorced. Bryce couldn't start over after his first overdose, continuing to return to addiction and homelessness. Alex couldn't start over after his decision at age six to end his life. Edward couldn't start over after the trauma from our childhood. Even Debby couldn't start over after her integration. She had to become yet another personality—Debby 2.

But I started over, reinventing myself multiple times. I chose vitality—a life of purpose and meaning. I saved myself. And I'm here to help others save themselves too.

CHAPTER THIRTY-THREE
VITALITY

With Jeff, I stopped being the caregiver. He showed me that it's safe to play another role, and he became my caretaker. After decades of being in charge of everything and everyone around me, this is now my daily practice: to be cared for and receive support. To be fiercely loved and protected.

Jeff takes care of our dogs and me. He takes care of our life. When the chronic Lyme disease acts up in my body, he puts me to bed, brings me food and supplements, and runs our household without my having to ask.

When I'm not sure about a business decision, he's right there with his excellent advice. When we're working on yet another house project, he's managing the contractors and dealing with our day-to-day reality.

When I don't know how to do something, he figures it out, because Jeff is the smartest person I know. When it's time to play, he's always up for new adventures. He calls me out when I need it, supports me when I need it, challenges me when I need it, and loves me when I need it. He helps me to manifest, because he is an excellent manifestor, and he always assumes things will work out for him.

He is the perfect husband for me. My friends and clients, when they hear about Jeff and everything he does for me, for our family, and for our community, comment on how lucky I am in love.

I am in love, yes, and it's lovely, but I'm not lucky and it wasn't luck that brought us together. I called him in. I was willing and able to receive the magnitude of Jeff's love for me, even when it scared me. I manifested Jeff because I was willing to be deeply uncomfortable. I was willing to be wrong about my assumptions of what a lifetime partnership looked like. I was willing to receive love in bigger and bigger ways. I was willing to get out of my own way.

When Jeff tells the story, he says that *he* called *me* in. After he set the three-mile radius on the dating app and stated his intention to only be on the app for three days, I was his first match. I let him say that. But he wouldn't have been able to do it if I hadn't been ready to be seen and loved.

Jeff loves showing off our home to others. He wants them to see how gorgeous it is. For years, I found myself holding back, letting him take the lead and downplaying the abundance that we have. But I've been learning something profound: My discomfort wasn't really about the wealth itself—it was about my deep-seated fear of being truly seen.

Growing up, I learned to make myself invisible, to shrink, to hide any sign that I might deserve good things. The message was clear: wanting beauty, comfort, or abundance made you selfish, made you "bad, rich people," like my parents warned against. But more than that, I learned that being seen meant being vulnerable to judgment, criticism, or abandonment.

Now, surrounded by brand-new dishes, a walk-in closet with its own library ladder, and a well-stocked pantry, I'm practicing something revolutionary: allowing myself to be witnessed in my fullness. I love being surrounded by beauty, and I'm learning that it's safe to let others see that I love it. This isn't about the material things themselves—it's about my willingness to be seen as someone who deserves good things, who has worked for them, who doesn't need to apologize for her success.

Jeff comes from wealth. He is comfortable with it. He expects luxury. Our private joke is that his biggest disappointment in childhood was that his mother wouldn't let his father buy a private plane for family adventures. That reality is so far from my childhood that it's hysterical to me every time he mournfully brings it up. But his ease with abundance has taught me something crucial: There's freedom in being unapologetically yourself, in letting people see all of who you are.

The journey from paralysis in choosing toilet paper to running a successful business took years of unlearning family patterns, not just around wealth but around worthiness itself. I'm still discovering how to be comfortable with my financial abundance, just as I help my clients navigate their own transformations. But more importantly, I'm learning how to be comfortable being fully seen in that abundance.

When I share my story now, when I let people into our beautiful home, when I speak openly about my success, I'm not just modeling financial recovery—I'm modeling the radical act of believing I *deserve* to be seen and loved exactly as I am. Because if my clients can see I once struggled with the same fears they have, if they can witness my learning to receive love and support without shame, they'll understand that healing doesn't require perfection. It requires courage to be witnessed.

I've learned that I deserve love and support as a natural expression of my wholeness. The abundance in my life—financial, emotional, spiritual—isn't something to hide from. It's evidence of what becomes possible when you stop making yourself small, when you allow others to see you fully, when you believe deeply that you are worthy of all the good things life has to offer.

This is what I want my clients to understand: Becoming whole means letting yourself be seen in your fullness—your struggles and your triumphs, your fears and your abundance, your journey and your destination. Because you cannot heal in isolation, and you cannot love yourself fully while hiding who you've become.

Through being married to Jeff, I am learning that it is safe to stop living a life of self-preservation. I have finally stopped surviving and begun thriving. My life looks radically different than the paths my immediate family chose. I believe this difference exists because I took 100 percent responsibility for myself, with no excuses, transforming my trauma into a teaching tool rather than a life sentence.

I built my dream business, helping other healers and leaders transform their own wounds into wisdom. I married my dream husband, who celebrates my success instead of fearing it. We built our dream home, a physical manifestation of the stability I never had growing up. I live my dream life—not by fragmenting like Debby's alters but by integrating all parts of myself. All the dreams, all at the same time. Vitality in action.

When you make a significant change like this and take 100 percent responsibility, I believe that you change seven generations behind you and seven generations in front of you. You literally put a ripple in the time-space fabric of everything that is happening. This isn't just about personal transformation—it's about healing ancestral wounds and creating new possibilities for those who come after us.

CHAPTER THIRTY-FOUR
MOM

Shortly after my 50th birthday, I received a letter in the mail from Debby, asking to be in contact. "I miss my daughter!" She was about to turn seventy-five and wrote that she has "no idea why we haven't been in communication all these years."

We'd exchanged no more than a few sentences for nearly fifteen years and were living radically different lives in different parts of the country.

I desperately wanted to ask her the question I have tried to resolve on my own for fifty years: "Of all of the personalities, who really is my mother?"

This is the question neither I nor my brothers were ever able to answer. I've never dared ask it because I don't know what I'll do if I discover that among the 123 personalities, I have no real mother.

What if feeling like a motherless child for the majority of my life isn't simply a case of traumatic circumstances but of calculated creation by a narcissistic captor? What if I was only brought into existence to fulfill Debby's obsession with being loved and adored?

I wrote back and suggested a phone call, stating that I had a few questions to ask about my childhood. Debby miraculously agreed, and I prepared no less than one hundred questions to ask, wanting to ensure no stone was left unturned.

I reviewed each question carefully with Jeff and my aunt. Together, we considered the best flow for the conversation. Should I start with softball questions, like, "Tell me about Dad's childhood" or "What positive memories do you have about us when we were little?"

Or would the conversation be cut short before I could get to more important questions, like about my being sexually abused or about how many times Debby attempted suicide?

I wrestled my need to manage Debby so she stayed on the phone with my own desire to ask the hard questions. If I pumped her too quickly for information or suggested she was an incompetent parent, she might not tell me anything. The conversation would be in vain, and I'd be right back to where I was before the call.

The night before we spoke, I dreamed that Debby and I were sitting in a truck stop, the kind with rows of gas pumps and enormous restrooms alongside fast-food chains and one family-style sit-down restaurant. This is the type of travel center you often find along long stretches of highway across the United States, where cars can pull in from either direction, allowing passengers to make a quick pit stop to pee and eat.

We are sitting in orange and yellow plastic chairs connected together along a wall in the center courtyard of this truck stop. Giant skylights hover above us, providing natural light. We watch people filter in and out of lines at the fast-food restaurants.

We're seated at a square, black, metal table with a brown laminate surface. Debby has an entire box of matches in front of her. Her latest suicide strategy seems to be setting herself on fire. I try to coax the matches away from her before anyone notices.

Then the scene shifts. We are in a family community center made from cement blocks in the middle of a cluster of cabins. Smells of mold and dankness fill the empty hall. It reminds me of our childhood basement.

The center has a low ceiling made of acoustical tiles, some splotched brown from water damage. Long, uncovered, flickering fluorescent lights hang from the ceiling by metal rods. There's a lopsided pool table, a foosball table missing three players—two blue and one red—and tattered badminton and croquet sets available for use on the unkempt lawn.

Two brown vending machines stand at attention in the far corner. My brothers are thrilled they can get orange soda in glass bottles and their favorite candy while they fight to win a game of foosball. The orange and yellow connected plastic chairs reappear along the walls of the community center.

The boys and I are all wearing short shorts—red with white piping at the edges—and graphic T-shirts from the thrift store with red piping around the edges of the sleeves. The boys wear matching tube socks and knock-off Converse All Stars. I'm wearing knock-off pink jelly shoes that I think make me look like a princess. Together, we create a fashion statement a decade too late.

The scene shifts again, and we're in a semi-rustic cabin in a wooded area. It's nighttime, and we're singing along to the one cassette my parents bring with us from home—Bruce Springsteen's Born in the U.S.A., played on a small boom box. We light a fire in the tiny fire pit outside the cabin and roast popcorn over the open flame.

Then, suddenly, it's morning, and just Debby and I are in the cabin. She is in the kitchen, swallowing a bottle of pills. As I slowly move toward her, I watch her fall to the floor and die.

I clean up the mess. It's important to me that there is no evidence of her death. I know what to do next. The brown glass pill bottle gets thrown away. The fading yellow laminate counters are wiped down to remove the pill residue. Her almost rigid body is removed from the house. When Dad and the boys get back from wherever they were, they don't notice that Debby is gone. They don't ask about her. That she ever existed has been completely erased from the family.

I woke up, drenched in sweat, tangled in the sheets of our marital bed. Jeff's hand pressed reassuringly against my back, where I often find it after I sleep fitfully. I reminded myself, as I do every morning, that *I am safe now.* I wondered why even in my imaginary dream state I chose to be the responsible adult in my family, cleaning up after Debby.

Later, I remembered that this cabin vacation did happen. It was in the early fall two years before Tracy died, when Debby was a few months pregnant with Edward, before our family's rapid decline began.

We could afford the trip because my parents got a significant discount for the cabin by renting it during the off season. Summer was over. Kids were already back in school. Since we were home-schooled, it didn't matter when we went on vacation. I remember it being lonely in the state park community center, with no other kids to play with.

The trip was before Debby became suicidal for a decade and before Dad started physically abusing us on a regular basis, when I still thought my family was safe and possibly even normal.

The phone call with Debby 2 took place later that day. Our conversation was stifled and tense. She wanted to discuss things like gardening and my dogs. I wanted to discuss why Child Protective Services (CPS) never came to our childhood home, which is where I began the conversation.

As usual, we were not on the same page.

Debby 2 said it was "pretty easy" for CPS to not get involved. Then she immediately changed her answer to "I don't know. I don't know." She said that Bryce and Alex were both seeing therapists as children, when they were suicidal, which is "all CPS would have recommended anyway."

I countered with, "I'm talking more about day-to-day support because you were suicidal for a decade. Dad was unavailable. I don't know if it's because we hid it so well, or because it was the 1980s and certainly a different time than how things are handled now. I'm so surprised that there was not any kind of formal intervention to make sure us kids were okay."

Debby 2 replied, "Well, you know, formal intervention would have told us that we needed to get therapy, which we did. The usual thing is for a family to pitch in, but I didn't have a family that was inclined to pitch in."

Ah, there it is. Debby 2 is conveniently the martyr and victim again, right where she likes to be. I can no longer blame her for her lack of parenting because no one in our family was supporting her.

I changed the subject. "Do you remember my taking Edward to high school with me for the day so I could take care of him when he was a baby and he didn't have childcare?"

Debby 2: "No. Was it Take Your Kid to School Day?"

Me: "No, that's not a thing. Students at my high school didn't have babies to bring with them to school."

I changed the subject again because we were obviously not going to make any headway on the topic of my parenting my brothers.

I brought up Dad. "Did you think or imagine that Dad's violence toward you would stop when you had children?"

Debby 2: "I don't think I thought about it at all. I really wanted children."

Once again, her needs supersede any concern about the safety of her own children.

Me: "But at what cost to you and your children?"

Debby 2: "That's a good question. I don't think I was thinking about that. I was so happy when I found out I was pregnant with you. It was so exciting."

Being reminded of how emotionally absent Debby was in my childhood has caused me to stop breathing. The air is stuck in my throat. Her ability to change the narrative from willing us into a world where we were not safe is replaced with her excitement about being pregnant. I know what my role is. I'm supposed to get on board with how excited she was to be a mother and be grateful that she wanted me. But I don't fall for it.

I change the conversation again. "How and when were you diagnosed?"

Debby 2: "By my first therapist and at the Psychiatric Institute of Washington by a therapist that specialized in MPD."

Me: "What caused the different alters to come Outside?"

Debby 2: "I never knew."

Me: "I have memories of playing with Alice and Five when I was four or five. We were playing dolls in my bedroom with a tea set."

Debby 2: "Well, I used to play with you kids a lot."

Me: "But this was not an adult version of you. This was a child version of you."

Debby 2: "Hmm … That's interesting." She had nothing more to say on this subject.

Debby 2 is incapable of acknowledging any moment in time when she was anything other than a dutiful mother and caregiver.

Me: "What do you remember about the alter Ten?"

Debby 2: "She was a tomboy, wasn't she?"

Me: "Ten had a lot of anger. Ten would get angry a lot."

Debby 2: "Oh, so that's where I put that. Hmm."

There is no recognition or acknowledgement of the terror that Ten caused me or my brothers.

Me: "There was a male alter too, who would pop Out occasionally. Tony was a grown-up guy from Brooklyn who always seemed surprised that he was dressed in women's clothing and had breasts. He tried to be the funny guy, staring down at your breasts, saying, 'Hey, whad I'm supposed to do wit' these?' Do you remember him?" I asked Debby 2, searching her voice for any flicker of recognition.

"I very, very vaguely remember him." Her voice trailed off, distant and uncertain. "I don't know. He was probably where I stuffed all my ideas of what it means to be a boy."

The clinical detachment in her voice makes my stomach clench.

"Yes," I pressed on. "He's the one who would hide your car keys all the time. Remember when he stuffed them between folded sheets in the linen closet?"

I'm fishing for acknowledgment, trying to prove to both of us that these memories aren't just mine to carry.

"Hmm."

The sound barely escapes her lips, a dismissive murmur that closes the door on further discussion. We might as well be talking about distant cousins from a forgotten family reunion rather than the multiple personalities who were as much a part of our daily life as breakfast or bedtime. These alters weren't just occasional visitors—they were the architects of our family's reality, the reason I learned to read facial expressions before I could read books.

I sit there, frustration burning in my chest, feeling slightly unmoored from reality. How can she be so casual about Tony, about any of them? These aren't characters in some half-remembered story—they were the reason I learned to keep spare car keys hidden in my sock drawer at fourteen, the reason I memorized different personalities' favorite foods and fears. Yet Debby 2 is treating them like faded photographs in an album she's barely interested in flipping through. I change the subject again.

Me: "Do you know which of the alters gave birth to the boys and me?"

Debby 2: "No, I remember those births. So maybe I wasn't splitting apart. I don't know. I don't understand it. Your dad was so excited."

She's back to focusing on the positive. I'm racing against time, trying to extract truth from between her carefully constructed deflections, knowing our window of honest conversation will slam shut the moment I refuse to participate in her revisionist history.

"Another thing you shared with me during that time," I ventured, measuring each word like medication, "is that your mother was part of a satanic cult and that cult also abused you."

Debby 2: "I don't remember that at all. Wait a minute. I'm sort of remembering. I think I made that up. That doesn't ring true." Her voice carried the careful distance of someone examining someone else's memories. "I mean, I'm sure I said it to you. But it doesn't ring true."

"That's a pretty extreme thing to make up," I observed, my voice steady despite the emotional earthquake rumbling beneath my words.

I recognize this pattern—the selective amnesia, the casual dismissal of extreme claims, the quick pivot away from uncomfortable truths.

"Yeah," she replied, and just like that, the door closed. Topic dismissed, memory erased, truth buried beneath another layer of denial.

This interaction exemplifies the challenges of healing generational trauma. When the keeper of family history constantly rewrites the narrative, how do we find solid ground for our own healing? When truth becomes as multiple as Debby's personalities, how do we build a foundation for recovery?

This conversation also highlights the painful paradox of seeking truth from someone who has mastered the art of forgetting. Like trying to catch smoke with bare hands, each attempt to grasp reality slipped through my fingers, leaving me with nothing but the lingering scent of what might have been truth.

Finally, remarkably, a few minutes later, when I mention Tracy abusing me, she said, "I'm so sorry I didn't protect you."

I don't know which alter said that to me because we are on the phone and I can't read her body language, my primary way of recognizing the alters.

I know I'm supposed to acknowledge Debby for having never sexually abused me. I should congratulate her for breaking the cycle of sexual abuse in our family. But I can't. I can't acknowledge her because I am too triggered.

Once again, I had no idea what was and was not real in our communication.

Seventy minutes into our seventy-five-minute conversation, I asked Debby my most important question: "Out of all of the personalities, who is our real mother?"

I waited for Debby 2—this supposedly "integrated" version—to respond with the kind of maternal warmth found in Hallmark movies. I can almost hear it before she speaks: "Well, of course it's me, sweetie."

The words would be perfectly scripted, perfectly appropriate, perfectly Debby 2, because that's her specialty now: performing the role of proper mother with the same dedication that once went into managing her personalities. She's traded multiplicity for a carefully curated singularity, exchanging the chaos of fragmentation for the precision of positive thinking. The irony doesn't escape me— how this "integrated" version of my mother has become yet another performance, another personality to add to the collection, this one specializing in appropriate responses and sunny dispositions.

In her quest to be the right kind of mother, she's become a character in her own play, delivering lines that sound like they've been focus-grouped for maximum maternal effect. It's as if she's studied a manual titled How to Be a Normal Mother *and is determined to ace the test, even if it means glossing over the decades when she was anything but.*

Even though it can be hard to know when Debby 2 is telling the truth or lying, I anxiously wait for an answer to my question. With her reply, my search for my mother's true identity will end. I can fill the gaping hole in my heart where my love for my mother is meant to live.

She said, "Debbie Sue."

POSTSCRIPT

Multiple personality disorder (MPD), now known as dissociative identity disorder (DID), is characterized by the presence of two or more distinct personality states that recurrently take control of the individual's behavior, accompanied by an inability to recall important personal information that is too extensive to be explained by ordinary forgetfulness. It is caused by severe physical, sexual, and psychological trauma, usually in childhood.[1]

The American Psychiatric Association officially recognized MPD in 1980. There was a considerable spike in MPD diagnoses in the 1980s, with people claiming to have been sexually abused as children. Thousands were diagnosed in that decade. By the 1990s, 40,000 people had been diagnosed with MPD in the United States. Some say this dramatic increase in diagnoses was due to increased recognition of the disorder, others say it was due to inappropriate therapeutic approaches.

Debby went to the Psychiatric Institute of Washington for evaluation and diagnosis in 1990. This is where she asserts that her 123 personalities were identified. In the 1980s and early 1990s, the Psychiatric Institute had an entire wing dedicated to the disorder. All of a sudden, it seemed like everyone around us was a multiple or knew about MPD. Books and movies like *Sybil* and the *The Three Faces of Eve* were popular during this time.

The 1980s also saw a seismic shift in how MPD was understood, largely due to Cornelia Wilbur's work with her famous patient Sybil.

---

[1] For more information on various aspects of MPD and DID, including how these disorders develop, their diagnosis, and their treatment, see "What Are Dissociative Disorders?" by the American Psychiatric Association, https://www.psychiatry.org/patients-families/dissociative-disorders/what-are-dissociative-disorders

Wilbur's influential theory linked MPD directly to childhood trauma, particularly severe abuse. This connection sparked a cultural phenomenon that merged with the era's mounting fears about satanic influence. As heavy metal music incorporated occult imagery and themes of devil worship, reports of ritual abuse began surfacing in MPD cases. The resulting narrative—linking MPD, childhood trauma, and satanic cults—spread through medical literature, media coverage, and therapeutic circles, creating a perfect storm of cultural anxiety and clinical theory. This convergence would later be scrutinized by researchers and clinicians, revealing the complex interplay between trauma, diagnosis, and societal fears. In 1994, an article in the *International Journal of Clinical and Experimental Hypnosis* stated that:

> During the past decade in North America, a growing number of mental health professionals have reported that between 25% and 50% of their patients in treatment for multiple personality disorder (MPD) have recovered early childhood traumatic memories of ritual torture, incestuous rape, sexual debauchery, sacrificial murder, infanticide, and cannibalism perpetrated by members of clandestine satanic cults. Although hundreds of local and federal police investigations have failed to corroborate patients' therapeutically constructed accounts... [it seems that these patients] have been caught up in social delusion.[2]

The decline of public fascination with MPD in the early 1990s stemmed from several converging factors. The sensationalized stories of satanic ritual abuse that had captured public imagination began facing increased skepticism from researchers and clinicians. Some highly publicized MPD cases were revealed to be either exaggerated or inadvertently influenced by therapists' expectations and questioning techniques.

---

[2] Sherrill Mulhern, "Satanism, Ritual Abuse, and Multiple Personality Disorder: A Sociohistorical Perspective," International Journal of Clinical and Experimental Hypnosis 42, no. 4 (1994): 265, https://doi.org/10.1080/00207149408409359

The 1994 shift to the term DID reflected a deeper understanding of the condition's nature. Rather than emphasizing the existence of separate, distinct personalities, the new terminology acknowledged that dissociation—the mind's ability to disconnect from overwhelming experiences—was the core mechanism. This renaming marked a move away from the dramatic, media-friendly narrative of "multiple personalities" toward a more nuanced understanding of trauma response and identity fragmentation.

The change also coincided with the mental health field's growing sophistication in understanding trauma's impact on the developing brain. DID began to be understood not as a mysterious phenomenon of multiplicity but as a creative survival strategy developed in response to severe childhood trauma—a framework that proved more clinically useful than the sensationalized MPD narrative of the 1980s.

It is now recognized that DID's dissociated states are not fully formed personalities but rather represent a fragmented sense of identity. The amnesia typically associated with DID is asymmetrical, with different identity states remembering different aspects of autobiographical information. There is usually a host personality who identifies with the person's real name. Typically, the host personality is not aware of the presence of other alters.

In Debby's case, many of her alters were aware of each other, and there did not appear to be a host personality. Unlike the way in which this disorder is typically portrayed in books and movies, there was no one core person who was Out most of the time, with other alters popping Out from time to time. Debby was constantly switching personalities, and even the personality who gave birth to me doesn't appear to be the host. This extreme version of multiplicity, essentially annihilating the host at a very young age, is uncommon. It is more common for a host to lie dormant for a period of time, sometimes even a few years, in order to protect it from abuse. But in Debby's case, there was likely never a clear host.

A few years ago I asked my aunt, Debby's older sister and only sibling, about whether she remembers Debby's original identity. She distinctly recalled Debby speaking in a variety of accents continuously throughout their childhood. She couldn't recall Debby having one clear personality that was Out most of the time.

The different personalities may serve distinct roles in coping with problem areas. An average of two to four personalities/alters are present at diagnosis, with an average of thirteen to fifteen personalities emerging over the course of treatment. Environmental events can trigger a sudden shifting from one personality to another.

With Debby, everything seemed to trigger the shifting. At least a dozen alters were present at her diagnosis, with the others discovered during treatment at the Psychiatric Institute of Washington. The final total was 123.

The cause for dissociation and splitting is most apparent to me as described in Onno van der Hart's structural dissociation model.[3] This theory explains how the minds of trauma survivors compartmentalize as a response to chronic trauma. The premise is that no one is born with an integrated personality. The brain comprises a number of discrete structures governing different functions that communicate via neural pathways. These pathways are called the "fault lines for dissociation."

The brain's natural architecture, with its distinct regions and neural networks, creates a blueprint for psychological separation when faced with overwhelming trauma. Like rooms in a house that can be closed off during a storm, this compartmentalization allows the mind to seal away traumatic experiences while maintaining function in other areas. This brilliant survival mechanism, which I witnessed firsthand through Debby's personalities and the "house" inside of her mind, enables the psyche to respond to danger with remarkable adaptability, protecting essential parts of the self while managing threats in the present moment.

I believe that it takes a certain brain capacity to develop distinct personalities, who may or may not know about each other. It's not

---

[3] For more on this model, see Onno van der Hart, Ellert R. S. Nijenhuis, & Kathy Steele, *The Haunted Self: Structural Dissociation and the Treatment of Chronic Traumatization* (W.W. Norton, 2006).

something everyone can do. These distinct personalities are developed in response to trauma. Each personality has its own traumatic experience(s), and it isolates itself into a separate personality as a way to protect the other parts of the personality from that trauma. Debby had so many traumatic events happen to her that she split into 123 personalities.

Dr. Janina Fisher, an international expert on the treatment of trauma, understands dissociation as adaptation.[4] Each part is designed to promote survival. As more compartmentalization occurs, parts develop with instinctive defense survival responses: flight, fight, freeze like a deer in the headlights, submit, cry for help, or attach for survival. This system of splitting maximizes survival chances by engaging multiple survival strategies simultaneously. For example, the submit part might caretake the abusive caregiver while the fight part remains hypervigilant, scanning for danger; the cry-for-help part tries to elicit support from other family members; and the flight part imagines a fantasy world of safety.

I can see these responses in Debby's different alters, and even in myself and my brothers. The flight response reflects being ready to run or distract, always ambivalent and unable to commit. Of Debby's alters, Anna's eating disorder and vague responses best exemplified this. My brother Bryce's drug use similarly represented this escape mechanism.

The fight response is characterized by intense hypervigilance and readiness for action. The alter Ten was quick to anger and always on guard. This is how I responded to trauma during Debby's suicidal years, numbing my own emotions to maintain vigil.

Freeze response is our internal alarm system, warning of danger through terror and paralysis. 24 lived on the edge of suicide, and my brother Alex would freeze when confronted, struggling to function in the adult world.

---

[4] Janina Fisher, *Healing the Fragmented Selves of Trauma Survivors: Overcoming Internal Self-Alienation.* (Routledge, 2017).

Submit response is characterized by depression, shame, and self-sacrifice. Debbie and Debby 1 both reflected this response: Debbie was the compliant caretaker. Debby 1 took the brunt of physical abuse from Dad. I self-sacrificed in an attempt to keep my family alive.

Finally, the cry for help response is seeking protection through innocence and dependence. Five and Alice, Debby's child-like alters, mirrored my youngest brother Edward's need for protection.

According to the American Psychiatric Association, suicide attempts and other self-injurious behavior are common among people with DID. More than 70 percent of outpatients with this disorder have attempted suicide, a statistic that became painfully personal during Debby's darkest years.

Treatment typically involves psychotherapy aimed at integrating the different elements of identity. With Debby, therapy made her much worse before she became better—an insight that now informs my trauma recovery work in teaching others that healing isn't linear and that much caution should be used in reliving traumatic experiences.

What I have learned over the years of studying this mental illness, both through personal experience and professional training, is that the people who create separate personalities in response to trauma are brilliant. It takes a remarkable mind to cultivate multiple realities, to teach itself to splinter off and separate in the face of abuse. I recognize that dissociation itself is a form of genius—a survival strategy that deserves respect even as we work to heal it.

Debby is one of the smartest people I have ever met. Her brilliance captivates those around her. She draws them in with her ability to manipulate any situation in her favor. Her extreme number of personalities speaks to her capacity to expand her mind to create new realities over and over again. Trauma responses, whether they're dissociation, hypervigilance, or withdrawal, represent not weakness but incredible strength and adaptability.

Are you impressed by someone who can speak a dozen languages? How about someone who can live a dozen lives? These questions have shaped my approach to trauma recovery, informing the creation of my online programs that help practitioners understand trauma not just as damage to be repaired but as evidence of the mind's remarkable capacity for survival.

Today, the Psychiatric Institute of Washington, DC, where Debby was officially diagnosed with MPD, no longer has any reference to MPD or DID on its website. The MPD treatment wing is gone. This once-popular diagnosis has all but disappeared from mainstream discourse, though its legacy lives on in the lives of survivors and their families.

In our last conversation, Debby 2 confirmed what I had long suspected: that her original identity, the person born as Debby, was not our mother. Instead, our mother, the only personality who felt responsible for parenting us, was the alter named Debbie Sue, who appeared fewer than a dozen times during our childhood. None of us have seen or spoken with Debbie Sue for over thirty years. She disappeared along with Debby's suicidal ideations in the mid-1990s. She was gone, and someone unidentifiable began walking around in Debby's body.

Several weeks after this conversation, Debby 2 emailed to say that she found our conversation too painful, and she doesn't want to speak with me again about my childhood or the alters. This final act of emotional avoidance exemplifies why I developed the four phases of trauma recovery in my work: rescue, recovery, reconstruction, and evolution. These phases emerged from my own experience of finding wholeness after fragmentation, of transforming survival skills into healing tools for others. Without moving through these phases, we remain trapped in our protective patterns.

The Rescue Phase: This phase focuses on stability, safety, and getting basic physical needs met. It reflects my immediate response to whatever crisis was presenting in that moment, where my survival instincts took over and I did whatever was necessary to stay alive. In this phase, I operated on pure adrenaline, my body and mind focused solely on making it through the next moment, the next personality switch, the next crisis.

The Recovery Phase: Mental and emotional trauma are identified and attended to in this phase. This is the phase where I began to process what happened, allowing myself to feel the emotions I couldn't during the crisis. I started to acknowledge the cost of survival, the pieces of myself I had to fragment or abandon to keep going.

The Reconstruction Phase: In reconstruction, healing becomes possible. Also known as the rebuilding phase, this is where I began to create new patterns and ways of being, which I now help others achieve through my trauma recovery work and through speaking and writing on mental, emotional, and spiritual resilience. Here, I learned to integrate my experiences, to build something new from the fragments of my past, to build a life beyond being the daughter of 123 personalities.

The Evolution Phase: In evolution, we become a new version of ourselves—more healed and whole. This phase was where my trauma became transformation, where I shifted from survivor to thriver. This is where I discovered that wounds can become wisdom, scars can become strength, and the past can become purpose. This is the journey I'm still on, helping myself and others find their way from fragmentation to wholeness.

My path from managing my mother's 123 personalities to serving as a trauma chaplain and ultimately developing trauma recovery programs taught me an essential truth—survival strategies, no matter how fragmented or complex, deserve our reverence. Debby's multiplicity was her mind's brilliant solution to unbearable pain, just as hyper-responsibility and extraordinary attention to detail were mine. Now, as I guide others through their own healing journeys, I honor both the wounds and the wisdom they carry. In every shattered story I encounter, I recognize echoes of Debby's creative resilience, of my brothers' quiet endurance, of my own transformation from surviving to showing others how to thrive. This is the ultimate gift of our family's fractured legacy: the understanding that within our deepest wounds lies the possibility for our greatest transformation.

CONTINUE YOUR HEALING JOURNEY

Use the QR code below to access resources to deeper healing and transformation beyond the pages of Emma's memoir.

Trauma Recovery Programs

At the heart of these resources are online trauma recovery programs utilizing the same four-phase methodology (Rescue, Recovery, Reconstruction, and Evolution) that Emma developed through her own healing journey.

Weekly Support and Practical Tools

Emma's "Letters from Resilience" newsletter is delivered every Sunday to thousands of readers worldwide. These weekly letters provide ongoing guidance, practical resilience tools, and inspiration drawn from Emma's work as a trauma recovery specialist and business coach. You'll also find access to Emma's curated reading list, book club discussion guides for deeper exploration of *Unshattered*'s themes, and additional books by Emma Churchman. Each resource is designed to meet you wherever you are in your healing journey, whether you're just beginning to understand your trauma or ready to help others navigate theirs.

Professional Development and Speaking Opportunities

For those called to bring trauma-informed approaches to their organizations or communities, the webpage details Emma's speaking and workshop offerings. As a nationally certified trauma chaplain and PhD candidate in Conscious Business Ethics, Emma presents to corporate wellness programs, healthcare organizations, educational institutions, and community groups worldwide. The site also provides information about limited private mentoring and executive coaching opportunities for qualified applicants.

Whether you're seeking personal healing, professional development, or organizational transformation, the link below serves as your comprehensive resource hub for turning trauma into triumph.

https://emmachurchman.com/unshattered

ACKNOWLEDGMENTS

To my brothers Bryce, Alex, and Edward—you are woven into every page of this story. I am living not just for you, but because of the love that connected us through our darkest moments.

To all of the alters who trusted me to witness your existence and honor your purpose—thank you for protecting our family in the only ways you knew how. To Debbie Sue, Anna, Five, and Debby 1 especially: I love you, I miss you, and I carry you with me always.

To my husband Jeff, whose unwavering belief in me gave me courage when mine faltered. Thank you for loving all of me. Your steady presence made healing possible.

To my aunt and uncle, who became my chosen parents and helped me piece together fragments of memory with patience and grace. Your love showed me what family could be.

To Don Ledbetter and Larry Easterling, my CPE supervisors, for recognizing that my deepest wounds could become my greatest ministry—and for guiding me with wisdom and grace as I learned to be fully present in others' trauma without losing myself.

To my writing team who transformed raw pain into purposeful narrative: Blaise Allysen Kearsley and Caryn Mirriam-Goldberg for coaching me through the craft; Sonia Castleberry for developmental editing that honored both story and healing; Laurie Knight for copyediting that preserved my voice while polishing my words; my beta readers for identifying the gaps that mattered; and Tascha Yoder for her brilliant ability to capture the essence of a story in its title.

To Mark Packard and Number Three Productions for masterful sound engineering and for understanding that recording trauma stories requires more than technical skill—it requires holding space with grace while someone speaks their deepest truths.

To Michelle Vandepas and GracePoint Publishing for recognizing that some stories need to be shared not because they're easy to tell, but because they're necessary to hear.

To all the children who grew up navigating a parent's mental illness—I see you, I believe in you, and I want you to know that your survival was not your only purpose. You were meant to thrive.

And finally, to every person who will read this book and recognize pieces of their own story—may you find in these pages not just validation for your pain, but permission for your joy.

ABOUT THE AUTHOR

Emma M. Churchman, MDiv

Emma M. Churchman, MDiv is a nationally certified trauma chaplain, leadership consultant and executive mentor who has spent over 25 years guiding individuals and organizations through the unspoken aftermath of trauma. With a rare blend of spiritual insight and strategic leadership, she has helped thousands transform pain into power—drawing deeply from her own harrowing journey through acute childhood adversity.

Emma is the founder of the *Trauma Recovery Certification Program*, a groundbreaking training for professionals who want to address trauma at its roots—not just manage symptoms. Her teachings are a bold invitation to rewrite the stories we inherit. Emma blends clinical understanding with soul-deep wisdom, making her a sought-after speaker for those ready to engage in real, raw healing.

Whether she's speaking to Fortune 1,000 leaders, faith communities, or trauma survivors, Emma teaches practical, evidence-informed trauma recovery techniques that empower individuals and organizations alike to reclaim agency, reconnect with their core selves, and navigate life's storms with integrity. As a PhD candidate in

Conscious Business Ethics, she bridges the gap between soulful leadership and actionable strategy.

From the serene mountain peaks of Gerton, North Carolina, where she lives with her husband Jeff and their dachshunds Winston and Leroy, Emma continues to inspire people to find strength, meaning, and hope—even in the darkest of times.

For more great books from Empower Press
Visit Books.GracePointPublishing.com

EMPOWER
P   R   E   S   S

If you enjoyed reading *Unshattered*, and purchased it through an online
retailer, please return to the site and write a review to help others
find the book.

www.ingramcontent.com/pod-product-compliance
Lightning Source LLC
Chambersburg PA
CBHW070059030426
42335CB00016B/1950